D1605489

Lost Cities of the Ancient Southeast

University Press of Florida

GAINESVILLE · TALLAHASSEE · TAMPA · BOCA RATON · PENSACOLA · ORLANDO · MIAMI · JACKSONVILLE

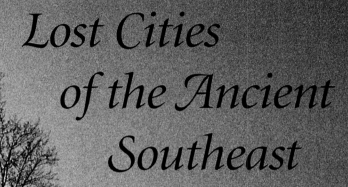

Lost Cities
of the Ancient
Southeast

Mallory McCane O'Connor

Site photographs by

Barbara B. Gibbs

Title page: Mound at Etowah. Photo by Barbara B. Gibbs.

Copyright 1995 by the Board of Regents of the State of Florida
Printed in the United States of America on acid-free paper ∞
All rights reserved
Designed by Louise OFarrell. Set in 10 pt. Minion.

00   99   98   97   96   95   6   5   4   3   2

LIBRARY OF CONGRESS CATALOGING-IN-PUBLICATION DATA
O'Connor, Mallory McCane.
Lost cities of the ancient southeast / Mallory McCane O'Connor;
site photographs by Barbara B. Gibbs.
p. cm.
Includes bibliographical references and index.
ISBN 0-8130-1350-X
1. Indians of North America—Southern States—Antiquities.
2. Mound-builders—Southern States. 3. Southern States—
Antiquities. I. Title.
E78.S65O36   1995   94-39265
975′.01—dc20

The University Press of Florida is the scholarly publishing
agency for the State University System of Florida, comprised
of Florida A & M University, Florida Atlantic University,
Florida International University, Florida State University,
University of Central Florida, University of Florida, University
of North Florida, University of South Florida, and University
of West Florida

University Press of Florida
15 Northwest 15th Street
Gainesville, FL 32611

To my parents, Kenneth and Lela,
who taught me to love the land

Contents

Illustrations

Preface

AMERICA WASN'T DISCOVERED IN 1492. It was discovered instead more than 20,000 years ago when Siberian hunters crossed the land bridge between Asia and Alaska and followed a path southward between the ancient glaciers into the heart of North America. These hardy immigrants were not searching for gold or seeking profitable trade. They were nomads, big game hunters, and over the centuries they pushed ever southward, following the herds. As their numbers increased they fanned out over the great expanse of virgin land and developed dozens of distinctive ways of living in their new environment. When the Europeans arrived in the "New World," some 20,000 years after the First Americans, they found the land populated by millions of inhabitants. In America north of the Rio Grande there were at least fourteen cultural groups speaking hundreds of languages. Throughout the eastern half of North America they found impressive commercial and religious centers, a vast array of beautiful objects created by skilled artisans, and an extensive trade network, which at one time covered an area larger than Western Europe. Agriculture, art, architecture, astronomy, commerce, religion—the Indians of the precontact era evidenced a sophisticated knowledge of each of these components of civilization.

Yet early European settlers arriving in North America believed that the land contained no civilization, and so they saw none. Upon visiting the fledgling United States in the 1830s, Alexis de Tocqueville wrote that North America was inhabited only by wandering tribes who had no thought of profiting by the natural riches of the soil and that the vast country was still, properly speaking, "an empty continent, a desert land awaiting its inhabitants" (de Tocqueville 1945).

De Tocqueville was wrong, yet his mistake is understandable. In the eastern half of the country especially, by the early 1800s, the great and mysterious civilizations of precontact times had vanished almost entirely, and the descendants of those great cultures, decimated and dislocated by three centuries of disease and warfare, were reduced to bands of refugees struggling to survive the onslaught of European colonization.

It has been over a century since the symbolic end of Indian resistance—

the massacre at Wounded Knee. The twentieth century has seen the fulfillment of the doctrine of Manifest Destiny and the development of America as an international superpower. At the same time, America's indigenous people have been reduced in the popular imagination to a romanticized stereotype—colorful symbols of a Wild West that has long since been conquered and tamed.

We stand now at the century's end, confronting a new millennium, and despite our apparent successes we are faced with difficult questions about ourselves as a people and a nation. We have built cities and railways and roads and dams. We have cleared the land and filled it with farms and factories, fought two world wars, and sent men to the moon. Yet we find ourselves facing an uncertain future, and as it becomes increasingly clear that our great natural resources are not infinite, that our grand technologies may not, in fact, provide the solutions to all our problems, we are beginning to question the wisdom of the path we have been following. We have taken our nourishment from the land on which we live, but can that nourishment be sustained indefinitely? We have put down roots in this New World, but we do not see the depth of our roots, and so we do not know the source of our nourishment (Weatherford 1991, 18).

To paraphrase historian Jack Weatherford, our cultural roots as Americans lie buried in the ancient mounds that dot the eastern half of the continent and in similar prehistoric sites and modern Indian reservations across the country. We have too long ignored the ancient cultures that helped shape our collective destiny. We have not acknowledged our debt to our ancestors. From the earliest times, Indian culture has manifested itself in the development of America—in our political life, our form of government, our economy, our food, our art, our agriculture, our language, our place-names, and our distinctly American modes of thought (Weatherford 1991, 18).

When the Europeans, and after them the Africans and the Asians, came to the New World as immigrants, they entered an ancient land already endowed with a rich cultural heritage, one that remains with us despite centuries of abuse and neglect. The Indians assisted the newcomers as guides, teachers, and allies, teaching them how to grow corn, how to survive treacherous winters, how to use plants to heal and to kill. Without the help of their Indian mentors, the early immigrants would never have survived in the perilous wilderness that confronted them.

As the settlers grew and prospered, they continued to borrow heavily from their Indian neighbors in the areas of language, architecture, and the arts as well as in medicine, law, and the natural sciences. Benjamin Franklin used the democratic structure of the Iroquois Confederacy as a model for the U.S. Constitution.

Lost Cities of the Ancient Southeast is a lesson in American history. It takes the reader on a journey of discovery to explore the ruins of Indian towns that were already hundreds of years old when Columbus first set foot on the sandy shores of Hispaniola. From the Indian city of Cahokia, the ancient capital of the American heartland, to the island stronghold of Calos, the king of the Calusa, near present-day Naples, Florida, *Lost Cities of the Ancient Southeast* examines the extent and significance of the artistic and architectural history of the ancient Southeast. Over twenty ceremonial sites are represented in the book along with the sculpture, engravings, ceramics, and other artifacts associated with each area. The text is supplemented by more than thirty site photographs by Barbara B. Gibbs, who captures the lonely beauty and quiet grandeur of the "lost cities of the Southeast." Line drawings and architectural plans of the sites by internationally known architect William Morgan help to point out the geometric elegance of precontact urban design. Maps of the southeastern region provide geographic orientation and clarify the interrelationship of the ceremonial centers with the riverine networks that connected them. By putting Indian art and culture into a specific geographical context, *Lost Cities of the Ancient Southeast* gives the reader a sense of place as well as an idea of the timeless beauty and technical sophistication of indigenous art and architecture.

American Indian art and architecture are embedded in the land. The sun, the sacred landscape, the elements of earth, air, fire and water, and the myriad creatures that inhabit our world are the basic components of an ancient and deeply spiritual way of looking at the world. At archaeological sites throughout the Southeast, the layout of cities, the choice of materials, and the artifacts associated with them all point to communities that were part of the natural environment and based upon the surrounding landscape. Indian societies were organized as an integral part of the structure and rhythms of nature, and this principle is visible in every aspect of Indian art and culture, from the great architectural structures of Cahokia to the humblest burden basket of a village farmer. In most of the Indians' origin myths, the People emerged from the *land itself*, and they are always part of it. The forces of nature were acknowledged and celebrated. Art and architecture were bound together in what art historian Richard Townsend calls "an intricate fabric of reciprocity, by which the people drew together the living, the dead, ways of subsistence, and the structures and rhythms of the universe" (Townsend 1992, 47).

This complex relationship between humankind and the land gave the American Indians a solid foundation on which to build a worldview that was linked to the past through a sense of place and a continuity of custom, and that extended into the future as part of the process of nature's cyclic renewal. Indian religions recognize the indissoluble connections among all living things and between animate and inanimate forms. They understand the vital importance of maintaining a harmonious balance between ourselves and the forces of nature, and they appreciate the consequences of being out of balance. The recognition of the interdependence of all forms of life is especially significant today as we face the ecological crisis of the coming decades, for not only does the Indian view bind human beings to the natural world; it also holds humanity responsible for the world's continued health. If we as a modern people can learn that lesson from our American Indian ancestors, if we can begin to see the world as they saw it by visiting their sacred landscapes and exploring their art and architecture, then perhaps we will be able to understand better our own place in the world and our duty to preserve the only source of our own continued well-being.

A BOOK IS LIKE A RIVER with many tributaries, each contributing to its development. This book began with a love of the land passed down to me from my Celtic ancestors that was reinforced by my earliest encounters with Native American culture. Two teachers in particular were early inspirations to me: Mary O'Toole, who presented a remarkably unbiased history of the California Indians to her fourth grade class, and Lucie Patton, herself half Navaho, who left a comfortable job in suburban Sacramento to teach on the Navaho reservation. I also want to acknowledge the influence of Jim Leedy, whose interest in Indian culture rekindled my own enthusiasm while I was an undergraduate at Ohio University, and Chuck Fairbanks, who introduced me to southeastern archaeology after I moved to Florida in 1969.

During the writing of this book, I received much appreciated assistance and encouragement from a number of individuals including my husband, John, my son, Chris, and my mother, Lela, and from my friends and colleagues in the Native American Art Studies Association, especially Amelia Trevelyan, Zena Pearlstone, and Janet Catherine Berlo.

This book was influenced by the work of many scholars, especially James A. Brown, David Penney, Jeffrey Brain, Vernon Knight, and Jack Weatherford. I also want to thank William Morgan, George Bedell, and Walda Metcalf for their continued encouragement and support. And, finally, many thanks to Barbara Gibbs, expert photographer and travel companion extraordinaire, for bringing my vision of the ancient Southeast to life.

Lost Cities of the Ancient Southeast

CHAPTER 1

Beginnings

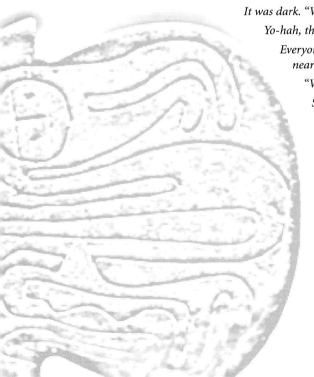

In the beginning, waters covered everything. Someone said, "Who will make the land appear?" Lock-chew, the crayfish, said, "I will make the land appear." He went to the bottom of the water and began to stir up the mud with his tail and his hands. He brought the mud to the surface and piled it up.

The beings who lived at the bottom of the water said, "Who is disturbing our land?" They kept watch and discovered the crayfish. But when they approached him, he suddenly stirred the mud with his tail so they could not see him.

Lock-chew continued carrying the mud and piling it up until at last he held up his hands in the air, and land appeared above the water.

The land was soft. Someone said, "Who will spread out the land and make it hard and dry?" Another said, "Ahyok, the hawk, should spread out the soft land and make it dry." Others said, "Yah-tee, the buzzard, has larger wings. He can spread out the land and make it dry and hard."

Yah-tee undertook to spread out and dry the earth. He flew above the earth and spread out his long wings over it. But after a while he grew tired of holding out his wings and began to flap them. In this way he caused the hills and valleys, because the dirt was still soft as he flapped his wings.

It was dark. "Who will make the light?" someone said.

Yo-hah, the star, said, "I will make the light."

Everyone agreed, and the star shone forth. But it was light only near the star.

"Who will make more light?" someone asked.

Shar-pah, the moon, said, "I will make more light." Shar-pah made more light, but it was still dark.

T-cho, the sun, said, "You are my children. I am your mother. I will make the light. I will shine for you."

The sun went to the east. Suddenly light spread over all the earth. As the sun passed over the earth a drop of blood fell from her to the ground. From this blood and earth sprang the first people, the children of the sun.

YUCHI CREATION MYTH

INDIAN ARTISTS of the ancient Southeast drew their subjects from the world around them—from the creatures of the air and earth and water whose strength and cunning the people observed and admired. The animals had preceded the First People. Before man arrived, the animals had ruled the world. These animals were the true ancestors, the ancient ones, and within them was to be found the wisdom of the ages. They were not put on earth to serve humans but rather to coexist with them within the complex and fragile balance of all life. It was only right that they should be revered.

In most of the southeastern Indians' creation myths there are three major players—the sun, the bird, and the water-creature (often the crayfish or the water spider). Fire, air, water, and earth are all represented in the origin of the cosmos, and each of these elements is represented symbolically in the religious iconography found on artifacts throughout the Southeast. The roots of these stories and their attendant symbols go back to a time before the arrival of the European invaders, to a time before the building of the great temple mounds, to a time when the ancestors of what would be the Hopewell civilization, one of the earliest great civilizations of the pre-Columbian era, were still living in the great northeastern forests. Throughout the rise and fall of civilizations, the passing of centuries, the sun, the bird, and the water spider were portrayed by the artists of the ancient Southeast. Like the serpent, the water spider and the crayfish are associated with water and fertility. They are equally at home in the water and on land. They represent the evolution of life from its watery origins to its emergence onto the land and into the air.

The metaphoric power of nature is evident in the images of the spider spinning its web, the panther stalking its quarry, the falcon displaying its dizzying prowess in airborne battle. These creatures are the subjects of myth and legend, the heroes of ancient tales, the helpers and tricksters who could either guide the way to prosperity and happiness or lead the unwary into certain disaster. The spiritual world was peopled by the ancestors of the animals. The spider, the falcon, the panther, the rattlesnake—these creatures and many more became symbols of honor and prestige, emblematic of social standing and ancestral heritage, heraldic creatures who symbolized a power far greater than that of their natural animal selves. Whether fashioned of clay, engraved on shell, cut from copper, or carved in stone, these creatures were the subject of an art that was rooted in the natural world but that imbued that world with a vision of magic and magnificence. They captured the spirit presence beneath the veil of illusion, the universal and eternal within the humble and the ordinary.

Who were the artists who created this distinctive and visionary body of work from the humblest of materials, whose eyes saw the eternal hidden within the temporal? Where did they live and for whom were these works created? What happened to these people and to the cities where they lived and worked, and what can they tell us about our world and our heritage, as Americans and as human beings?

We can search for the answers to these questions in several ways. We can look at the "facts" as we understand and define them—at dates, chronologies, statistics, analysis of materials, stratigraphy, maps, charts, and historical precedents. These pieces of information add to our understanding of that long-ago world and the people who inhabited it. They allow us to draw on our own knowledge of history and to make comparisons and analogies, to see similarities between the civilizations of the pre-Columbian Southeast and those of, say, Mexico or Egypt.

But even more important to our understanding is the less tangible structure that holds the facts together, the space that lies between the particles of fact, the glue that holds the pieces in position. In order to understand the art and architecture of the ancient Southeast, we will need to penetrate the surface and immerse ourselves in a different way of seeing reality, a different interpretation of the "facts," for we do not see with the eyes of the ancient ones. We have had different teachers and have been taught to look for different information. It will take a leap of imagination for us to be able to understand a worldview that is alien to our own, to suspend our prejudices and preconceptions and see the world with new eyes. But that is what we must do.

Consider, for example, the sacred mountain. Since the beginning of history, people the world over have looked upward, toward the sky, for inspiration and assistance. "I will lift up mine eyes unto the Hills from whence cometh my help." In the ancient Tigris-Euphrates valley, the Sumerians built their ziggurats, artificial hills topped with dwelling places for their gods. In the great valley of the Indus River, the earliest civilized peoples of India erected stupas, holy mountains that rose toward heaven. The pharaohs of Egypt commanded their royal architects to design huge pyramids. Thousands of slaves toiled year after year to create mountain tombs worthy of a Royal God. The sacred mountain links heaven and earth, provides access to the Deity, elevates some above others. As it was in Sumeria and Harappa and Egypt, so it was in southeastern North America.

There are, however, important conceptual differences between the beliefs attached to the pyramids of Egypt and those associated with the mounds of North America. To the American Indians, the sacred mountain and the four sacred directions provided the conceptual framework for architectural design. Primal architecture is ritualistic architecture. It grows and develops out of the land itself, a manifestation of ritual rather than of individualized planning. It is not meant to aggrandize the ego of the ruler or the architect but rather to fulfill the requirements of the supernatural forces that control the world. It is a collective expression of anxiety and hope, a tangible record of a collective concept of reality.

In 1539, Hernando de Soto and a company of soldiers landed in Florida and marched northward, looking for gold. Scattered throughout the land were numerous towns and villages, many of which were reported to have one or more mounds topped with temples and the dwellings of chiefs and nobles. Garcilaso de la Vega, the Inca historian who chronicled the de Soto expedition, wrote:

> The Indians of Florida always try to dwell on high places, and at least the houses of the lords and Caciques are so situated even if the whole village cannot be. But since all of the land is very flat, and elevated sites which have the various other useful conveniences for settlement are seldom found, they build such sites with the strength of their arms, piling up very large quantities of earth and stamping on it with great force until they have formed a mound from twenty-eight to forty-two feet in height. Then on the top of these places they construct flat surfaces which are capable of holding ten, twelve, fifteen or twenty dwellings of the lord and his family and the people in his service, who vary according to the power and grandeur of his state. In those areas at the foot of this hill, which may be either natural or artificial, they construct a plaza, around which first the noblest and most important personages and then the common people build their homes. (Varner and Varner 1980, 171)

The Europeans who settled in the Northeast did not at first find much evidence of the mounds that the Spaniards had described, but once they began to press westward, across the Alleghenies and into the Ohio and Mississippi river valleys, suddenly the mounds were everywhere. Large and small, solitary or in clusters, mounds dotted the landscape and bordered the rivers. In the Ohio Valley alone were 20,000 of these earthworks. But unlike the mounds of the Southeast, which were still in use when de Soto passed through in the mid-

1500s, those of the Midwest—of Illinois, Ohio, Indiana, Missouri, Kentucky, and Tennessee—were deserted, abandoned, overgrown with shrubbery and trees. Who had made them? And where had their makers gone?

The local Indians offered no explanations. They used the mounds as bases for their own village structures and were often familiar with the idea of a village laid out around a central plaza, but they had not made the mounds and, when questioned, spoke vaguely of the Old Ones Who Had Gone. The centuries of war, disease, and displacement that had followed the European intrusion into the New World had shattered the history of an entire civilization. The mound-building people, despite their knowledge of engineering, their understanding of astronomy, and their rich cosmology, did not, as far as we know, develop a written language, so they left no written history to document their beliefs and accomplishments. They cannot, then, speak for themselves except through the material culture that they left behind.

It is not surprising, then, that for nineteenth-century Americans, myths filled the vacuum left by lack of solid information. As Robert Silverberg pointed out in *The Mound Builders,* "Men in search of a myth will usually find one" (Silverberg 1970, 10), and during the nineteenth century the myths of the Moundbuilders were almost as numerous as the mounds themselves. Hebrews, Greeks, Persians, Vikings, Hindus—all were credited at one time or another with the construction of the American mounds.

It was not until the 1890s that the impressions recorded by de Soto and his contemporaries reemerged to put to rest the elaborate fantasies that had grown like tangled vines over the vestiges of the Lost Civilization. Major J. W. Powell wrote in the 1890–91 Smithsonian Institution's Annual Report of the Bureau of Ethnology:

> For more than a century the ghosts of a vanished nation have ambuscaded in the vast solitudes of the continent, and the forest-covered mounds have been usually regarded as the mysterious sepulchres of its kings and nobles. It was an alluring conjecture that a powerful people, superior to the Indians, once occupied the valley of the Ohio and the Appalachian ranges, their empire stretching from Hudson Bay to the Gulf, with its flanks on the western prairies and the eastern ocean; a people with a confederated government, a chief ruler, a great central capital, a highly developed religion . . . all swept away before an invasion of copper-hued Huns from some unknown region of the earth, prior to the landing of Columbus. (Silverberg 1970, 195)

But perhaps it was not simply "alluring conjecture" after all. The major flaw in the popular myth of the Lost Civilization of America was not its vision of vanished grandeur but the refusal to believe that the historic Native American tribes were the descendents of the Old Ones Who Have Gone, the builders of the great mounds. As art historian Cecelia Klein has pointed out, "In cases where murder and genocide were the practice, if not the policy, of the invader, natives were/are often portrayed by the aggressor as evil, unworthy, and deserving of elimination" (Klein 1990, 107). If the early European settlers found it difficult to believe that the "murderous, red-skinned savages" obstructing their Christian occupation of the wilderness were the heirs of a grand and noble civilization, we have today the opportunity to set the record straight.

The Moundbuilders were far from a vanished race; they were rather the ancestors of a people who, for a variety of reasons, had abandoned the old ways, losing the impetus, as well as the opportunity, to maintain the ancient monuments and continue the ancient faith. Times change. Needs change. Rome's decline was due as much to internal dissolution as it was to external conflagration. Civilizations follow the path from birth to death that affects all living things. The time of the mounds had passed, but the people had remained.

IT WAS MORE THAN a single cycle of rise and fall that produced the mounds that dotted the southeastern landscape. There had been several waves of moundbuilding activity over a period of 3,000 years. One of the earliest examples, dating from circa 1500 B.C., is found at Poverty Point, near the present-day town of Floyd in West Carroll Parish, Louisiana, where a cluster of six mounds is located (see figure 1).

The Poverty Point mounds were first noted by archaeologists in 1872, but they received little attention until the mid-twentieth century when the U.S.

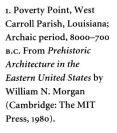

1. Poverty Point, West Carroll Parish, Louisiana; Archaic period, 8000–700 B.C. From *Prehistoric Architecture in the Eastern United States* by William N. Morgan (Cambridge: The MIT Press, 1980).

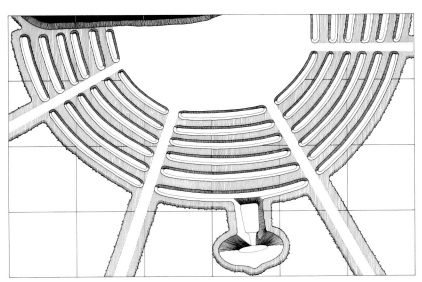

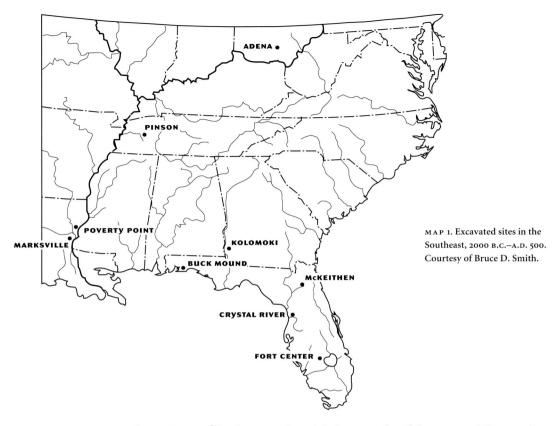

ADENA •

PINSON •

POVERTY POINT •

MARKSVILLE •

KOLOMOKI •

BUCK MOUND •

McKEITHEN •

CRYSTAL RIVER •

FORT CENTER •

MAP 1. Excavated sites in the Southeast, 2000 B.C.–A.D. 500. Courtesy of Bruce D. Smith.

Army Corps of Engineers took aerial photographs of the group while mapping the Mississippi River. In 1953, these photos were studied by James A. Ford, then on the staff of New York's American Museum of Natural History. Ford noticed an unusual geometrical arrangement no one had detected before. It seemed to him that the worn ridges of the Poverty Point mounds had originally formed octagonal blocks made up of six concentric rows of mounds separated by outward radiating aisles. At some distant time in the past, a shift in the channel of the Arkansas River must have washed away the octagons' eastern sides. A report that Ford and C. H. Webb published in 1956 estimated that the original mound group may have been 11.2 miles long, six feet high, and eighty feet wide. This would equal some 530,000 cubic yards of earth, they calculated—thirty-five times the volume of the Great Pyramid of Khufu in Egypt. The largest mound of this structure, Ford wrote, "is easily the most spectacular of the accomplishments of these people. It measures 700 by 800 feet at the base and rises to 70 feet above the surrounding plain. . . . It can be estimated that the finished mound required something over three million man-hours of labor" (Ford and Webb 1956).

Further study revealed that the huge complex had been built in a single effort over a relatively short period of time, and Ford estimated that it must have taken about 20 million fifty-pound basketloads of earth to complete the work. He concluded that "this community must have been rather strictly organized. While a religious motivation may ultimately explain the large amount of earth construction, this effort was obviously well controlled. The geometrical arrangement of the town . . . [is clearly the result] of central planning and direction" (Silverberg 1970, 196).

Based on our knowledge of history and the conceptual framework of our Graeco-Roman heritage, we might be tempted to look to Rome or Egypt for analogies, to see elite masters cracking whips over the backs of pathetic slaves as they struggled to fulfill the grandiose visions of ambitious and despotic rulers. But these analogies do not fit the evidence that has slowly emerged from the ruins of the Moundbuilders' widespread civilization. The story that emerges is perhaps even more startling, telling of a widely scattered and diverse population, loosely knit kinship societies seemingly egalitarian in social structure, who were inspired by a set of spiritual concepts to participate in the construction of vast earthworks meant to acknowledge not earthly kings but the powers that controlled the universe. The building of the mounds was, then, an "act of faith" necessary to ensure the welfare of all the people.

Scholars originally thought that Poverty Point had been a distant colony of the Adena-Hopewell civilization that dominated the Ohio River Valley, and most of the Eastern Woodlands, between 700 B.C. and A.D. 400, but carbon-14 dates for material recovered from the Poverty Point site placed it as much as 600 years earlier than the first Adena sites. It seems impossible that such vast works could have been constructed by a pre-agricultural people who had not even developed pottery, yet no traces of agricultural activity have been found at the site and the only ceramic works, besides a few small figurines, are clay balls that were probably used to line cooking pits.

It is tempting to look to Mexico as a source of inspiration for the developments at Poverty Point, and there are some parallels, to be sure, but no material evidence has yet been discovered to support more than a tenuous connection. So far, Poverty Point appears to have come independently into being toward the end of the North American Archaic tradition, a transitional period of adaptation and development that began around 8000 B.C.

It is most interesting that at Poverty Point the huge bird-shaped effigy mound located to the west of the series of concentric octagons is positioned to provide a clear view of the sun rising over the center point of the octagonal formation at the exact time of the spring and fall equinoxes. Whether this siting was deliberate is unknown, but later examples of sophisticated "calendar circles" that may have served to mark the dates for planting and harvest have been well documented throughout the Americas. The creation of such a device by a nonagricultural people would be unusual but understandable. After all, the seasons of the year, the availability of game and wild plants, are all governed by the movement of the earth around the sun. Even hunters and gatherers could profit from a certain knowledge of the changing seasons.

Or perhaps there were other reasons to chart the sun's journey across the heavens. In many times and places, people have attributed to the sun the status of a divine being. According to the accounts of European visitors in the seventeenth century, the Great Sun, chief of the Natchez, referred to himself as the child of the sun, claiming his right to rule based on his descendancy from the Divine Sun. Perhaps the people of Poverty Point acknowledged in their religion the significance of the sun's role in determining their own well-being. To be able to predict accurately the movements of the Bringer of Life and Light would certainly offer some sense of security to a hunting and gathering people.

Myth, ritual, architecture, art—these were the tools through which the people could relate to their environment and secure their survival. Thus, as Arnold Rubin has pointed out in his book *Art as Technology,* art was not viewed as a commodity by the people of pre-Columbian America, or even as a category of objects created to give aesthetic pleasure. Art served more crucial functions. It helped to establish the parameters of individual and group identity, acted as a major means of enculturation for members of the group, and was also a form of *technology*—a technique for coping with survival, a tool for securing the blessings of health, abundance, and spiritual power.

The artist, in such a context, was not the pawn of wealthy patrons, expected to provide status-enhancing luxuries and aesthetic pleasure, or an alienated outsider, a disenchanted prophet bent on criticizing the status quo. The artist was, instead, a shamanic *technician,* one who could manipulate material elements that often contained great supernatural power. The artist was an essential component of the community whose work contributed to the orderly and effective functioning of communal life (Rubin 1989, 20).

And the art itself was in many cases an object of power, a repository for spiritual energy that could be used to benefit the individual and the larger community. Thus, the shell gorget worn by the Mississippian warrior was not just a piece of jewelry or even a badge of status or kin affiliation; it was in fact a statement of belief, an acknowledgment of participation in a whole system of social and religious patterns common to the entire culture.

THE FIRST GREAT MANIFESTATION of Native American art in the Southeast coincides with what scholars refer to as the Late Archaic period (3000–1000 B.C.). Several regional trade networks developed during this period, giving artists access to a wealth of exotic materials. The material recovered from the

Poverty Point site illustrates the extent of the trade network in Late Archaic times, for the inhabitants were importing flints, cherts, and copper from the north, steatite from the Appalachians, and a variety of valuable minerals, including galena, hematite, sandstone, jasper, and slate. A sophisticated lapidary tradition developed at Poverty Point in the making of effigy pendants and highly polished red jasper beads that often took the form of animals. The Poverty Point people also created the first known human figurines in North America. Made of clay, many of them portray pregnant females, suggesting some association with fertility (Penney 1985, 26).

One of the largest Late Archaic sites is in present-day Kentucky. Called Indian Knoll, it is located on the banks of an extinct channel of the Green River. Nearly 55,000 artifacts have been recovered from the site, including tools, weapons, ceremonial equipment, beads, pendants, and other ornaments. Some of the most exquisite objects found at Indian Knoll are the birdstones and bannerstones—worked pieces of slate, standstone, or other stones that may have been used as weights for balancing the hunter's *atlatl,* or spear thrower. Despite their small size, these objects have an elegance of form and finish that testifies to their makers' sensitivity and sophistication. Exquisitely functional, they are also beautiful by twentieth-century standards. Those who made them took great care to utilize the natural striations of the stone to emphasize their shape and enhance their aesthetic appeal.

The attention given to these objects is of interest, for unfinished stones of the same weight could just as easily have been attached to the spear-throwing device to balance it. Perhaps the formal qualities of the object, its appearance and finish, were important not for their own sake but because they enhanced the spiritual power of the object. Beauty was part of the plan of the universe, part of the harmony to be found in nature. A seashell does not need to be beautiful in order to provide a home for a sea snail, yet shells abound in exquisite color, graceful shape, and elegant surface detail. The artist must have looked to the natural world for clues to the dynamic power of nature, and the artist saw harmony, balance, theme and variation, modulation, intricate detail. The artist followed nature's lead.

Pottery also made its first appearance in North America (north of Mexico) during the Late Archaic period. A coarse, undecorated ware tempered with vegetable fibers has been found associated with early settlements at Stallings Island in the Savannah River Valley of southern Georgia. A similar fiber-tempered ware appeared along the St. Johns and Indian rivers in Florida around 2000 B.C. These simple, functional ceramics provided the basis for the development of elaborate ceremonial pottery embellished with incised designs, symbolic motifs, and painted decoration. Ceramic effigies and pipes were later added to the artist's repertoire.

Sometime shortly after 500 B.C., the diverse ceramic and ceremonial traditions evident in the Archaic period began to coalesce into four specific cultural complexes located along major river valleys in Tennessee, Illinois, Ohio, and Alabama/Mississippi. Interaction between these distinct cultural areas gave rise to what is called the Woodland period (500 B.C.–A.D. 500). There is no sharp break between the Archaic and Woodland periods; many of the political and social institutions established during the Archaic continued to grow and develop. What was new and significant in the Woodland period was the proliferation of mound-building practices and the extent and quality of ceremonial artifacts associated with those practices. It was as though a new religious fervor swept through the land, firing the people's imagination and igniting a dynamic chain reaction that resulted in a groundswell of mound-building activity. What was this new religion?

Some scholars have suggested that the introduction of agriculture into eastern North America was responsible for the dynamic changes that took place during the Woodland period. However, although the practice of cultivating certain crops for food had begun in eastern North America by about 2000 B.C., agriculture apparently did not become economically and socially significant until after A.D. 700, when maize cultivation became widespread. Throughout the Woodland period, hunting and gathering, supplemented by only marginal agricultural activity, continued to be the mainstays of survival. In contrast to the elaborate, hierarchical cosmology of the later Mississippian agriculturalists, the religious structure of the Hopewellians appears to have remained primarily kinship-based, with the natural world supplying the basis for myth and symbol. As with earlier hunter-gatherers, the Hopewellian worldview celebrated the power and mystery of the animals—a major source of sustenance for both the body and the imagination.

One plant that was cultivated throughout the period was tobacco. Tubular tobacco pipes, which began to appear during the Late Archaic and Woodland periods, show a stylistic progression toward greater elaboration and size (see figure 2). Indeed, pipes provide some of the most powerful examples of Woodland period art. Used ritually by most Native Americans of the historic period, tobacco may have played a role in the development of a ceremonial system that began to take root throughout the eastern United States. Certainly, the tobacco pipes created during the Woodland period were not intended for mere recreational use. In many cases they were so large and so heavy that it is almost impossible to think of them as mundanely functional.

The Adena culture of the Ohio River Valley was certainly the most elaborate of the Early Woodland societies. Material from most Adena sites dates from 1100 B.C. to A.D. 700. Like the Poverty Point people, the Adena people were moundbuilders. A great concern for the treatment, and perhaps the

2. Raven-effigy platform pipe, conglomerate, Rutherford Mound, Hardin County, Illinois; Middle Woodland period, 200 B.C.–A.D. 200. Courtesy of the Illinois State Museum, Springfield.

propitiation, of the dead led them to construct earthworks that often reached an impressive size—sometimes exceeding 100 feet in diameter. Gorgets of polished stone or copper, stone and fired-clay pipes, copper bracelets and rings, cut-mica ornaments and alligator teeth have been found associated with Adena burial mounds. Although ceramic vessels were produced by the Adena people, they were not apparently interred with the dead, although they may have been used in graveside rituals (Brose 1985, 53).

Early investigators proposed that Mexico was the likely source of Adena cultural traits, basing their theory largely on the mound-building activity, which, they pointed out, might well be derived from Mexican prototypes. They suggested that Poverty Point could have been the first manifestation of a new civilization moving out of Mexico and up the Mississippi River Valley into the American heartland. This is a nice, neat theory, but it is not supported by the facts. There is no clear-cut migratory path, no evidence of Mexican-manufactured artifacts at Poverty Point or in any Adena sites, and no early chain of mounds linking the Gulf Coast to the Midwest.

More recently, scholars have been studying sites in the Northeast and the Great Lakes for signs of Adena origins, and here the facts seem to offer more conclusive evidence of a connection. Although the Archaic people of the Northeast did not build mounds, their burial customs were similar to those of the Adena people, and they may have served as an early prototype for the development of Adena ideas.

3. Wilmington tablet, sandstone, Late Adena culture; Middle Woodland period, 400 B.C.–A.D. 1. Photo from The Detroit Institute of Arts; courtesy of the Ohio Historical Society, Columbus.

The stone pallet, or plaque, is considered to be characteristic of the Adena cultures. Stone tablets existed throughout eastern North America during this period, but the Ohio examples are especially intriguing (see figure 3). David Brose wrote in an essay on Woodland art, "A small group [of tablets] from the Ohio Valley is engraved with designs composed of broad lines that may be interpreted as highly stylized raptorial birds. . . . The traces of pigment on these tablets suggest their use as stamps, possibly for decorating perishable organic materials such as cloth or the walls of houses. Similar carved representations appear on a bowl cut from a human skull unearthed at the Adena mound in Florence, Ohio" (Brose 1985, 53).

Pipes provide us with the most elaborate examples of Adena art, and one of the most interesting is a unique human-effigy pipe discovered in Ross County, Ohio (see figure 4). The pipe, about ten inches high, represents a standing male and is the only known human subject portrayed by an Adena artist. The figure is posed in a rather awkward partial crouch, knees bent, hands held stiffly at his sides, wearing a breech cloth with a curvilinear design, an elaborate headdress, a feather bustle, and large earrings or "earspools" that project outward from the sides of his head. The details of his face are carefully depicted, with well-defined eyebrows, cheekbones, nose, and chin, but his eyes

4. Human-effigy pipe, pipestone, Adena Mound, Ross County, Ohio; Early Woodland period, 500 B.C.–A.D. 1. Courtesy of the Ohio Historical Society, Columbus.

are open and staring and his mouth frozen in a grimace or shout. While Adena representations of animals were usually lively and naturalistic, this depiction of a human being is stiff and formal. Does he represent a shaman? A dwarf? A departed spirit or ancestor? There is something otherworldly about him, something preternatural that places him outside the realm of everyday experience. It is also possible that this unique artifact was produced outside the area, for in terms of form as well as scale it bears little resemblance to other pipes of local manufacture.

The pipe-carving tradition was one of many cultural traits that carried over into the Middle Woodland period, of which the Ohio Hopewell is the most spectacular example. Most Hopewell sites date from between 100 B.C. and A.D. 600, thus overlapping the Adena culture, from which they apparently borrowed extensively. Alternatively, it has been suggested that the Hopewell did not "succeed and supplant" the Adena, but that Adena and Hopewell customs developed side by side, enriching and enhancing each other's distinct cultures.

By A.D. 500, the Adena culture had spread all along the tributaries of the Ohio River, from southeastern Indiana to western Pennsylvania. Hopewell's sphere of influence was at that time more compact, centered primarily in the Scioto Valley of Ohio. The monumental system of mounds and earthworks clustered along the Scioto River are among the most impressive and perplexing of Ohio Hopewell phenomena. "Geometric earthworks occur as squares, circles, octagons, ellipses, and trapezoids. . . . They may be isolated, arranged in sets . . . or arrayed in complexes. There are also isolated examples of irregular or of stylized zoomorphic ones. The earthworks, which cover areas ranging from two to 1,320 acres in size, may be mathematically precise or rather careless in appearance. Many display an extraordinary correspondence of alignments, suggesting seasonal solar and/or lunar orientations" (Brose 1985, 65).

After some period of parallel development between the two cultures, Adena influence began to dwindle while the Hopewell culture flourished and spread. An abundance of grave goods have been found in conjunction with Hopewell sites—earspools, breastplates, gorgets, and headdresses made of copper; mica plaques and cutouts representing birds, serpents, profiled human faces, and human hands. Hundreds of pipes, most executed in a remarkably naturalistic style, have also been retrieved. Many of the pipes take the form of animals: birds (especially raptorial birds, including the peregrine falcon), frogs, bears, beavers. Their elegance and grace are disarming, attesting to the artist's powers of observation and indicating great technical skill. We know from historic accounts that pipes were prized among the Native Americans, and the sharing of a pipe was a time-honored way of signaling friendship and conciliation, an act of intimacy and mutual understanding.

Beautifully sculpted stone and ceramic pipes were not confined to the Ohio River Valley. Hundreds of miles to the west, in what is now southern Illinois, the people of the Havana culture were also making exquisite carved pipes representing a variety of birds and animals, while to the south, in Alabama and along the Gulf Coast, large steatite pipes in the form of falcons, owls, and panthers were being produced by the Copena culture (see plate 1). These pipes became a popular trade item after the first century A.D. and were exported to Illinois, Indiana, Ohio, and other locations throughout the Midwest.

The Hopewell people were the first great cultural tradition in pre-Columbian North America. Hopewell influence was widespread and had an enormous impact on the development of Woodland culture throughout the eastern half of the continent. The Hopewell people also continued the extensive trade network that brought them copper from the Great Lakes, mica from the Appalachians, volcanic glass from the Rockies, conch shells from the Gulf Coast, grizzly bear teeth from the Rockies, and a host of other exotic materials, most of which seem to have been used exclusively for the production of ceremonial and burial objects.

A preoccupation with death and burial was a salient feature of Hopewell life, and the construction of mounds appears to have been tied to an intricate set of rituals and ceremonies intended to protect the living, honor the departed, and ensure their comfort in the hereafter. Robert Silverberg, in *The Mound Builders,* calls the Hopewell "the Egyptians of the United States," pointing out that a single burial mound in Hamilton County, Ohio, contained "12,000 unperforated pearls, 35,000 pearl beads, 20,000 shell beads, and nuggets of copper, meteoritic iron, and silver as well as small sheets of hammered gold, copper and iron beads, and [many] other things as well" (Silverberg 1970, 218). But where are the towns? Where are the storehouses for agricultural surplus, the roads, the other attributes of civilization?

Scholars have struggled for years to explain the nature of Hopewellian society. Surely, they have contended, these people must have been agriculturalists. How else could they have supported the building of massive earthworks, the production of exotic artifacts? Yet archaeological evidence has revealed only scattered examples of organized crop growing, and the mound sites themselves have yielded little evidence of permanent habitation. The village sites that have been found are small and unimpressive, little more than a few huts inhabited by seminomadic hunters and gatherers who grew a few crops on the side. Even more curious is the fact that none of the villages were located near the large mound complexes. Perhaps these complexes functioned specifically as ceremonial centers, housing only a resident group of religious specialists and their families.

Adena mound sites were characterized by slow stages of construction over many generations as new burials were added layer by layer. The Adena people had lived near their mounds and had a close relationship with them over many centuries. But most Hopewell mounds were built in a single stage. Apparently, on certain ceremonial occasions, the Hopewell leaders sent out a call for participation. People throughout the area responded by coming together for a period of time to create the great earthworks, after which they returned to their distant villages to continue their seminomadic lives. Perhaps the Hopewell were not so much a political entity as a loose confederation of indigenous people who shared a common belief system and acknowledged a common spiritual leadership.

But where did their leaders come from, and where did they get their ideas? Most scholars agree that Hopewell culture began about 500 B.C., reached a peak around 100 B.C. to A.D. 200, and then slowly declined until it disappeared around A.D. 600–700. In searching for prototypes for Hopewellian culture, scholars once again looked toward Mexico. Although agriculture was not widespread during Hopewell times, knowledge of agricultural techniques was not entirely lacking. It is also possible to find other cultural traits—such as building large earthworks and producing certain ceremonial items such as mica silhouettes, earspools, and painted pottery—which may have some connection with Mexico. It was thought that the Crystal River culture, whose sites are found along Florida's Gulf Coast from Tampa to the Apalachicola River, might provide a link between Mexico and Hopewell sites to the north.

The major site at Crystal River, four miles from the Gulf, dates from circa 540 B.C. to about A.D. 1. It includes two large temple mounds with ramps, a small residential mound, two burial mounds, and a plaza (see figures 5 and 6 and plate 2). Archaeologist Clarence B. Moore excavated the main burial mound and its surrounding platform in 1903 and 1906, discovering 411 burials and a rich collection of shell ornaments, copper objects, and other artifacts. Later, this culture was shown to extend over a broad stretch of Florida. Many of its traits seem clearly akin to those of late Hopewell.

While mutual diffusion between coevally evolving centers is a better explanation than direct intrusion, some scholars have suggested that the Crystal River people were in direct contact with the Mexican civilization centered around Veracruz. Traders or colonists might have crossed the Gulf of Mexico and landed on the Florida Gulf Coast, inspiring the local inhabitants to mimic their descriptions of the splendors of their native land. The pair of incised stone columns found at Crystal River have been cited as evidence of possible contact between the Florida inhabitants and visitors from Mexico. However, the columns were found to have been carved around A.D. 440—too late to have had any direct influence on the Ohio Hopewell. Scholars continue to disagree on the plausibility of the Mexican connection, some pointing to

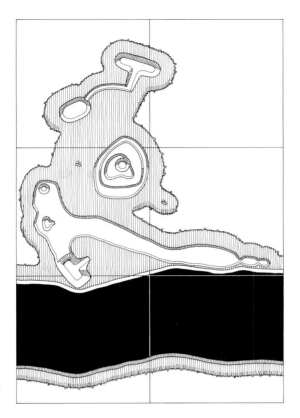

5. Crystal River site,
Citrus County, Florida,
200 B.C.–A.D. 1400. From
*Prehistoric Architecture
in the Eastern United
States* by William N.
Morgan (Cambridge: The
MIT Press, 1980).

6. Crystal River mound,
Citrus County, Florida.
Photo by Barbara Gibbs.

certain similarities in myths as evidence of strong cultural ties between Mesoamerica and points north, others citing a lack of conclusive evidence of contact other than sporadic encounters.

Other Florida sites of the Hopewell period, such as Fort Center, near the Everglades, have yielded a fascinating array of grave goods and ceremonial art (see figure 7). Mounds in a variety of shapes and sizes reveal a great range of burial customs. Fort Center included a wooden platform constructed over a pond, where it appears that bundles of bones were stored in preparation for burial at a later time. The platform was decorated with posts and lintels carved in the form of birds and animals that stood like guardian angels around the deposit of sacred bones. Farther to the north, sites along the St. Johns River also yielded carved wooden sculptures of birds, hinting at a rich tradition of wood carving throughout pre-Columbian Florida (see figure 8).

In contrast to later midwestern developments, south Florida never did develop a strong agricultural base. In this respect, Florida art and ceremonialism retained a number of Hopewellian elements far longer than was the case in other parts of the country. The Hopewellian pattern of a ceremonialism derived from or pertaining to supernatural relationships with animals continued to provide a basis for Florida's art long after it had been modified in other areas of the Southeast. As Hopewell influence declined after A.D. 500, these traits coalesced into a distinctive cultural pattern known as Weeden Island.

One of the most impressive Weeden Island sites is found at Kolomoki in southwestern Georgia, not far from the Florida border (see figures 9 and 10, plate 4). Here a group of mounds was constructed around a large open plaza, including a large flat-topped mound that once had a significant structure on its top. A number of striking ceramic effigy vessels were retrieved from the Kolomoki site, including two human effigies of kneeling men dressed in bird costumes (see figure 11). These effigies may be related to the "falcon-impersonator" that was to appear later in conjunction with the Mississippian culture. A number of zoomorphic ceramic effigies also discovered at Kolomoki represent opossums, doves, ducks, and panthers (see figure 12). Elegantly simple and beautifully decorated with incised designs and cutout patterns, these effigies are impressive evidence of the artistic excellence to be found in the pre-Columbian Southeast.

The most spectacular effigy vessel so far found in conjunction with a Weeden Island site is a masked figure recovered from the Buck Mound, a Weeden Island period mound located in Fort Walton Beach, Florida (see plate 3). The vessel, fifteen inches tall, is covered with red paste and painted with black and white decorations. The face resembles a mask, flattened and simplified, with wide-open staring eyes and a football-shaped mouth with prominent teeth and ears conventionalized into simple scrolls. The figure wears a red

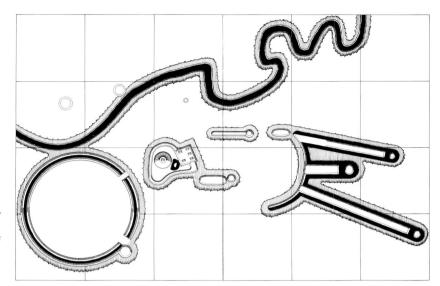

7. Fort Center site, Glades County, Florida; Belle Glade phase, 500 B.C.–A.D. 500. From *Prehistoric Architecture in the Eastern United States* by William N. Morgan (Cambridge: The MIT Press, 1980).

8. Charnel house post with eagle-effigy, wood, Fort Center site, Glades County, Florida; Belle Glade phase, 500 B.C.–A.D. 500. Courtesy of the Florida Museum of Natural History, Gainesville.

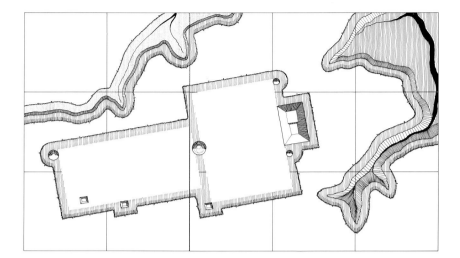

9. Kolomoki site, Early County, Georgia; Kolomoki culture, A.D. 600–900. From *Prehistoric Architecture in the Eastern United States* by William N. Morgan (Cambridge: The MIT Press, 1980).

10. Burial mound, Kolomoki Mounds near Blakeley, Georgia. Photo by Barbara Gibbs.

and white cape that has been incised with depictions of feathers. The presence of feathers further implies that the Buck Mound figure may be another early manifestation of the bird-man, or falcon-impersonator, a figure of great importance to Mississippian cosmology. Because of the unique characteristics of this vessel and the high quality of its construction, there has been some speculation regarding its origins. A thriving trade network existed throughout the Southeast, making it difficult for scholars to determine accurately whether artifacts were manufactured locally or imported from elsewhere. However, the discovery in the Fort Walton area of a number of bird and animal effigies that

11. Human-effigy figure, ceramic, Kolomoki site, Early County, Georgia; Kolomoki culture, A.D. 500–800. Courtesy of the Georgia Department of Natural Resources, Atlanta.

are similar in form and decoration points to the conclusion that the Buck Mound effigy was locally produced.

The end of the Hopewell culture is as mysterious as its beginning. By A.D. 550 the Hopewell people had stopped building ceremonial centers. In another two centuries their distinctive way of life had disappeared, and what was left of their culture had been absorbed by local groups. The debate continues regarding the cause of their demise. Was there some enemy—external or internal— that disrupted the structure of their world? Why did the trade network, which had supplied the raw materials so important to Hopewell civilization, collapse? What causes a culture as vital and successful as the Hopewell to dwindle and disappear?

But the mound-building impulse, although largely dormant for the next several centuries, remained. Hopewellian influence lingered in the outlying regions, and remnants of the civilization may have spread to numerous groups throughout the Southeast. Effigy mounds, built in the form of animals and

12. Opossum-effigy, ceramic, Kolomoki site, Early County, Georgia; Kolomoki culture, A.D. 500–800. Photo copyright Roy C. Craven, Jr.

birds, were constructed here and there. Some of the old ways and the old stories probably survived in myth and remembrance, and around A.D. 1000, some four hundred years after the end of the Classic Hopewell period, a new group of moundbuilders emerged. Once again great ceremonial centers were constructed; a highly stratified social structure developed; art and technology flourished. The cycle of the seasons of civilization turned once more, and ideas and energies that had disappeared for four centuries came again to life, growing and coalescing into a grand new cultural complex that would rival, and often surpass, Hopewell at its finest.

Although based in part on the Adena-Hopewell tradition, the new civilization would soon prove to be quite different—more organized, more highly structured, and more stratified. Rooted in the past, it would bring about a new, different array of art styles and belief patterns. Within a few centuries, the Mississippian way of life would be the prototype for people throughout the Southeast; the first, and greatest, city of this emerging civilization we call Cahokia.

CHAPTER 2

Cahokia

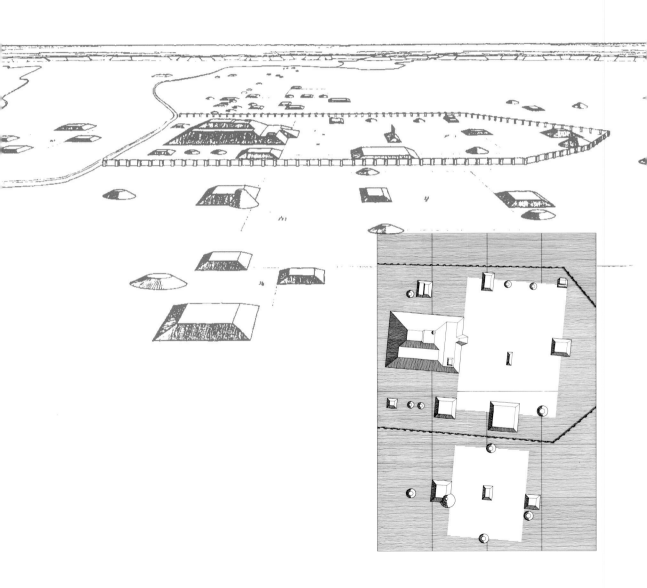

ANYONE WHO STANDS on the top of Monks Mound, a hundred feet above the surrounding plain, can see for miles in every direction. The flat, level heartland of the American Midwest rolls away gently to distant horizons, smudging into violet haze at the point where the sky meets the earth. To the west, beyond the broad, silver ribbon of the Mississippi River, is the present-day city of St. Louis, its skyline a flat, cardboard cutout of vertical rectangles slashed dramatically by the St. Louis Arch, symbolic gateway to the western frontier. To the north is Horseshoe Lake, a small artificial reservoir created by the damming of Cahokia Creek, a tributary of the nearby river. To the east, the rolling hills of southern Illinois recede into mist. And to the south lie the ruins of Cahokia—the grandest city of ancient North America, an imposing arrangement of mounds and plazas surrounded by a great stockade (see figure 13). Here lay the seat of power and authority that once controlled the lives of as many as 40,000 residents.

Founded circa A.D. 600, Cahokia grew, over a 400-year period, from a tiny farming hamlet to a burgeoning town. The rulers of Cahokia exerted their power over four concentric spheres of activity: the ceremonial complex of temples and burial mounds; the city itself, six and a half square miles, the Greater Cahokia area, which included suburbs and the rest of the American Bottoms along the Mississippi; and an extended sphere of influence that may have stretched as far north as the Great Lakes and as far south as the Gulf of Mexico.

The layout of a city—the orientation of the public buildings, the size and location of open spaces, the attention paid to private residences, the tombs of civic and religious leaders—tells a good deal about the people who live there, and the town plan of Cahokia is a beautiful example of the metaphoric power of architecture (see figure 14). At the city's center stands an enormous pyramidal mound (see plate 5). Called Monks Mound after the French Trappists who lived at the site in the 1800s, Cahokia's great mound was constructed over a period of three centuries and went through fourteen different building phases.

13. (top) Cahokia site, view from the west, Collinsville, Illinois; Cahokia culture, A.D. 900–1200.
14. (bottom) Cahokia site, main plaza, Collinsville, Illinois; Cahokia culture, A.D. 900–1200. From *Prehistoric Architecture in the Eastern United States* by William N. Morgan (Cambridge: The MIT Press, 1980).

By around A.D. 1150, the mound extended some 1,080 feet in length, was 710 feet wide, and rose 100 feet above the surrounding plain, covering sixteen acres at its base. A structure that sat atop the mound was more than 100 feet long and estimated to be at least four stories high—a major architectural achievement even by today's standards. Traces of a clay floor, support posts a foot in diameter, and walls three feet thick suggest a building about the size of a basketball court. Based on similarities with other Mississippian towns mentioned in the early accounts of European explorers, this impressive structure probably served as the temple/palace of the reigning chief.

The Monks Mound overlooked an enormous plaza, one of six major plazas within the city limits (see figure 14). These large, open spaces seem ideally suited to community gatherings and were likely the site of a variety of activities including religious celebrations, festivals, markets, and games that were important within the sociopolitical life of the community. A steep stairway led from the top of the mound to the north side of the plaza. To the southwest of the mound, about halfway across the plaza, stood a relatively small rectangular mound, known today as Mound 72, which was overlooked entirely when professional surveyors first mapped the mound site in the 1960s.

However, Melvin Fowler's 1973 excavations proved the significance of this unobtrusive earthwork, where he discovered evidence of some 300 burials and several caches of grave goods, including 455 beautifully worked flint arrowheads, 700 bone arrowheads, 36,063 marine-shell beads, and a number of ceramic vessels. Many of the skeletons interred in the mound were apparently sacrificial victims—most of them young women—who either chose, or had been chosen, to accompany the dead leader into the afterlife. The bones in Mound 72 lend credence to earlier theories about Cahokian social customs based on historical accounts of other southeastern Indians. They also provide graphic testimony that the rulers of Cahokia probably had the power of life and death over their subjects.

At the south side of the plaza stood two other large mounds that figured prominently in the life, and death, of the community (see plate 6). One of the mounds had a flat top that served as a base for the charnel house, or funeral parlor, where the honored dead were taken in preparation for burial. Members of the elite were apparently buried with, or near, the Great Chief himself. Their bodies were given a preliminary burial, after which the bones were disinterred, cleaned, and packed into bundles to await a second burial. Thus, another specialized occupation would have been that of "mortician" (probably a religious specialist) who acted as a caretaker of the elite remains.

Beside the charnel house was a conical burial mound where members of the aristocracy found a final resting place. That the Monks Mound faced these mortuary structures across the open plaza gives us some insights into the juxtaposition of life and death seen by the Mississippian people and their public acknowledgment of both the beginning and the end of the life cycle.

Initially, the ceremonial complex was not physically divided from the rest of the town. However, sometime in the thirteenth century, a massive stockade was erected around the plaza and the approximately sixteen mounds that comprised the political-religious core of the city (see plate 7). Fowler's excavations indicate that the job was done quickly, with residences and workshops evacuated on extremely short notice. "In some places," Fowler writes, "houses were abandoned with everything in them, pottery and flint artifacts left in place. You get the feeling that people had been living in the houses until just before the demolition work started, that they were there—and suddenly they weren't" (Fowler 1974).

The stockade was made of logs about the size of telephone poles. At regular intervals along its length there were towers with raised platforms from which defenders could launch arrows at attackers. The wall extended nearly two miles and required some 15,000 logs, a massive public works effort. The reason for fortification remains unclear. There is no sign of invasion, no evidence of great battles or wholesale massacre. Perhaps new people had moved into the area and had begun making surprise raids on the Cahokian farmers. Or, maybe the wall was constructed to keep dissatisfied Cahokians of the underclasses out of the inner city—to prevent an internal revolt of the disenfranchised majority.

Beyond the ceremonial complex (and probably at several other sites around the city) was another remarkable architectural feature that provides insight into the Mississippian lifestyle—a "sun circle." Excavations show that a quarter-mile-long circle of forty-eight logs set vertically into the ground was built to the west of the Monks Mound, just outside the stockade. Labeled Woodhenge by archaeologists, it may have functioned as an astronomical observatory that allowed Cahokians to record sunrise and sunset times and to determine the dates for plantings, harvests, and other ceremonies throughout the year.

Also outside the palisade were more than eighty additional mounds and five more plazas, which together covered more than six square miles. Lakes and streams dotted the landscape and may have been connected by canals. According to John Pfeiffer, in "Indian City on the Mississippi," "The traffic moving along these canals, and along waterways leading to remote sub-centers and outposts, may well have been heavy and regular. Historical accounts tell of 50-foot canoes carrying tons of goods, and the city must have had a small fleet of such vessels, together with auxiliary vessels and docks and boat yards" (Pfeiffer 1974, 137).

The fertile fields that surrounded the area, and the advancement of agricultural technology, contributed to the city's success. If Cahokia was not exactly the Rome of its day, the capital city of a far-flung empire, it was at least the hub of a vast trade network that spanned the eastern half of the continent. And, if not all roads led to Cahokia, at least enough of them did to make it a significant force in the dissemination of goods and ideas for a period of close to 300 years.

The roads, however, were made not of bricks but of water, and the warriors and traders who followed them traveled not by chariot but by dugout canoe. Cahokia was a river city, occupying a strategic location near the confluence of the Mississippi, Missouri, and Illinois rivers, and because rivers were the main avenues of transportation in ancient North America, it was in an ideal position from which to facilitate the commercial activity of the entire region. By the eleventh century, Cahokia was a thriving center of commerce from which the rulers controlled the distribution of raw materials—seashells, flints, copper, and mica—to its many satellite communities. By then, Greater Cahokia already included several suburban areas, two of them close to the heart of the city. A chain of mounds extended westward from the edge of the inner city through a six-mile-wide swampy region to the banks of the Mississippi River, where a cluster of twelve to fifteen mounds were constructed. On the opposite side of the river, where St. Louis stands today, another mound complex included a mound that stood fifty feet tall and covered a city block. This pair of mini-towns on either side of the river, linked directly to the main part of Cahokia, allowed for constant supervision of river traffic. Thus, every trader who used the major north-south highway of the continent had to pass through Cahokia's "toll booth" on the way up- or downstream.

Soon other satellite towns sprang up at strategic points along the Mississippi River: at the mouth of the Missouri, a route to the Great Plains, and at the Meramec, which led to the Ozark Mountains. Still others grew up along trade routes to the east. Sites as far north as present-day Wisconsin began to exhibit such Cahokia-like traits as pyramidal mounds and arrowheads and pottery of probable Cahokian manufacture.

Along with controlling a vast trade network, Cahokia was involved in the manufacture of goods and materials for export. Salt, obtained from a site some fifty miles from the city, seems to have been a highly prized commodity in ancient America and was a major Cahokian export. Stone hoes, made from grey-blue flint from a quarry at Mill Creek, a hundred miles southeast of the city, were manufactured in Cahokian workshops and became a familiar item throughout the entire region, apparently highly prized for their workmanship and efficiency.

In addition to such functional commodities as salt and tools, Cahokian workshops also turned out an array of exotic goods, such as stone pipes and ceremonial knives. Not only were these objects prized for their beauty and durability, they were also necessary for the maintenance of the Mississippian way of life—a life-style rooted in a system of rank and privilege based on religious traditions and inherited obligations. Evidence points to the existence at Cahokia of specialized workshops that produced exotic goods and suggests the existence of a class of artists who worked under the auspices of the political-religious leaders. These artists may have been part of Cahokia's middle class and, along with merchants, traders, and warriors, may have used their creative talents as a means of raising their social standing. Thus, a talent for carving stone or decorating pottery may have been one avenue of upward mobility in a society closely controlled by a ruling aristocracy. Alternatively, the role of artisan may itself have been hereditary, since the right to handle or possess certain spiritually powerful materials (copper, for example) was, among historic southeastern tribes, frequently based on family affiliation.

A rich agricultural base, a growing population, a concentration of political and religious power, a resident upper class who had the means and the desire to acquire objects of status, a lively commercial scene, access to trade and transportation—all served to make Cahokia a cosmopolitan capital, and it is in such an environment that art has traditionally flourished. Art in Cahokia was no exception.

In many ways, Mississippian art is an outgrowth of the Woodland tradition, and many components of the Adena-Hopewell heritage were retained well into the Mississippian period. Especially apparent throughout the Southeast is the persistence of a keen capacity for observation and an appreciation of the organic and volumetric aspects of the subjects represented. This trend may have reached its height during the late Woodland period in the graceful bird and animal sculptures created by the Hopewell in the Ohio River Valley area and the more exotic, but equally sensuous, Weeden Island ceramic pieces. This tradition of naturalism continued into the Mississippian period, but a shift in emphasis is almost immediately apparent: whereas the vast majority of Woodland art dealt with animal or bird images, much Mississippian art deals with human or quasi-human subjects or with anthropomorphized creatures such as the falcon-impersonator. From the start, then, Mississippian art is generally more anthropomorphic, more concerned with human subjects than Woodland art ever was. Just as Cahokian architecture mirrors a new stratification of society and the increasing complexity of religious ideology, so Cahokian art deals with new subjects and ideas while retaining a largely traditional approach to techniques and materials.

Some of the new subjects depicted by Mississippian artists were creatures of the imagination, fantasy animals or composite beasts that may have symbolized new religious concepts or illustrated emerging myths and legends. V. J. Knight, Jr., in his essay "Some Speculations on Mississippian Monsters," points out that the proliferation of unnatural subjects in Mississippian art—subjects such as antlered rattlesnakes with wings and human heads—may have resulted from the deliberate mystification of religious symbolism by the emerging Mississippian elite to "consolidate power by exhibiting a positive control over a scarce commodity, namely, esoteric knowledge" (Knight in Galloway 1989, 206).

According to Knight, in pre-Mississippian animal symbolism a selected natural species came to represent a variety of social distinctions. Whatever the specific social distinctions these ritual animals represented, the artists drew upon the observed world of nature to represent certain aspects of human society. While there are a few examples of fantasy and composite creatures found in Adena and Hopewellian art work, most of the animals portrayed are real animals and are generally portrayed realistically. Sociologists have pointed out that in societies that are undergoing a transformation into stratified hierarchies with political bureaucracies, emerging elites tend to consolidate power by achieving control over the use and distribution of limited resources, including specialized or esoteric knowledge. Seen in this light, the "new art" introduced during the emergent Mississippian period did not need to rely on external prototypes (such as images imported from Mesoamerica) in order to respond to the new political realities of social stratification and the "new religion" that supported it. It is, therefore, not surprising to find new subjects emerging, created to conform to a new pantheon of supernatural heroes and mythological monsters.

It was, however, humankind, in a newly broadened context and within a new conceptual framework, that became the most innovative subject of Mississippian art, and it was the concerns closest to the human heart—food, shelter, reproduction, relationships, family history and status, the meaning of life (and death)—that provided the basis for an explosion of visual imagery. The themes of fertility, warfare, and the honored dead, themes established during the Woodland period, were expanded during the Mississippian phase to reflect the increasing importance of agriculture and social stratification.

Much of our information about the ancient people of North America—their architecture, their religious and political institutions, and their social structure—is based on the accounts of early European explorers who visited the Southeast, beginning with Hernando de Soto in the mid-1500s. The remarkable writings of such men as Garcilaso de la Vega, the illegitimate son of an Inca princess and a Spanish conquistador who chronicled the wanderings of the de Soto expedition, Antoine la Page du Pratz, a Dutch settler who lived for eight years among the Natchez of southern Mississippi, and Jean Penicaut, a French ship's carpenter who came to the New World with Iberville and visited the Natchez in the 1700s, are rich sources of information. Although these accounts are often skewed by secondhand information or ethnocentric assumptions and thus are not totally reliable, they are, nevertheless, the best means we have of forming a three-dimensional picture of the lives of the precontact people of the Southeast. Archaeological data provide us with materials, dimensions, statistics, but if we are to put "flesh on the bones" the eyewitness accounts of those who experienced the last vestiges of Mississippian society in action are not to be totally discounted. Since much of the Mississippians' material culture was destroyed by war, displacement, and the ravages of time, and since the Mississippians themselves left no written records, the accounts of early historians and adventurers, however skewed, are useful in helping to fill the gaps between hard science and romantic conjecture. We must, however, try to avoid reading in too many of our own preconceptions. Cecelia Klein writes, "Native Americans, like so many colonized peoples, were variously equated by Europeans with barbarians, infidels, women, sodomists, and children. Once the trauma of conquest was behind them, however, Europeans began to construct more positive associations. The American Indian was often idealized, if not idolized, as the Noble Savage, the [indigenous] counterpart of members of Europe's highest social class. Post-Conquest New World [peoples] logically responded to this European concern with social class by emphasizing, if not exaggerating, even constructing, their own hierarchies and nobility" (Klein 1990, 107). Thus, the reader educated in the Western European tradition looks at Mississippian society and sees "class structures" and "social hierarchies" that may or may not be valid descriptions of the type of social structure characteristic of the Mississippian community. With that disclaimer in mind, we can examine the accounts of European contact with the southeastern people in a spirit of open-minded inquiry for the important information that they *can* convey.

Early in the seventeenth century, a French priest, Father Jacques Marquette, made a trip along the Mississippi River not far north of where Cahokia had been located. There, between the mouths of the Missouri and the Illinois rivers, he encountered a remarkable and terrifying sight, which he recounted as follows, "While Skirting some rocks, which by Their height and Length inspired awe, We saw upon one of them two painted monsters which at first made Us afraid, and upon Which the boldest savages dare not Long rest their eyes. They [the monsters] are as large As a calf; they have Horns on their heads Like those of a deer, a horrible look, red eyes, a beard Like a tiger's, a face somewhat like a man's, a body Covered with scales, and so Long A tail that it winds all around the Body, passing above the head and going back between the legs, ending in a Fish's tail" (Thwaites 1959, 139–41).

What the good Father saw was apparently a painting of a *piasa,* the dreaded Uktena or Underwater Panther that appears in the mythology of many eastern Indians. The painting has evidently long since disappeared, but his account of it serves to verify the potency of this ancient symbol well into postcontact times.

Water monsters hold a special position in southeastern mythology because although they are associated with the Underworld, they are also the guardians and controllers of life-giving water and thus are positively connected to both the world of men and that of the heavens. The piasa theme was utilized extensively in Mississippian art in works of many media and was pictured in many variations, including the winged rattlesnake with a cat's head and the panther with serpentine scales, both of which appear on shell engravings from the Spiro site in eastern Oklahoma. Despite its fearsome appearance, the piasa was connected with the positive aspects of water and fertility, both of paramount importance for an agricultural people.

It is not surprising, then, that one of the most powerful images found in the area of Cahokia depicts a serpentine creature with the head of a cat (see plate 8). Called the Birger figurine after the owners of the farm on which it was found, this statue depicts a kneeling woman using a hoe to cultivate the back of a coiled serpent. The woman is leaning forward as though straining with effort, and her left hand grasps the coiled body of the snake just behind its head. The head of this monstrous snake has panther-like characteristics, including a flattened muzzle and feline teeth. Gourd-bearing vines grow from the serpent's body and twine upward to the woman's shoulder. Why gourds, instead of the great Mississippian staple, corn? Archaeologist James Brown suggests the following: "Descendants of this species [of gourd] were among the earliest cultivated plants in the eastern United States. Originally the seeds were probably the object of cultivation. Subsequent selection for fleshy fruit led to the modern pumpkin and related squashes" (Brown 1976, 126). Indeed, gourds are said to "furnish the womb in which all more elaborate agricultural systems developed" (Lathrap 1977, 719), and may have been cultivated in North America as early as 3000 B.C. Perhaps, then, the Birger figurine represents an ancient agricultural entity who originally brought the art of cultivation to the people of the Mississippi Valley, an old mythological concept that preceded the introduction of maize agriculture. She may also provide the basis from which the Corn Mother mythology developed during the later, full-scale agricultural period (Emerson 1982, 10).

A second female statue from the same area, the Keller figurine, may indeed be associated with corn, for she is depicted kneeling in front of what is likely a metate, or grinding stone (see figure 15). The woman wears a short skirt and calf-length moccasins, and her long straight hair is pulled back from her face and falls to below her waist. She kneels on a mat that seems to be made of ears of corn, and the metate and stand that sit before her might also be interpreted to symbolize a cloud with falling rain.

Both the Birger and the Keller figurines are made of bauxite, a reddish-brown stone found in abundance in Arkansas, Georgia, Alabama, and Missis-

15. Keller figurine, bauxite, BBB Motor site, Madison County, Illinois; Sterling phase, Cahokia culture, Mississippian period, A.D. 1000–1250. Courtesy of the Illinois Department of Transportation, Springfield.

sippi. Since bauxite is not to be found in the southern Illinois area, it seems likely that the two female figurines were either manufactured farther to the south and imported into Cahokia or that the stone was imported and the statues carved in Illinois. Both figures are relatively naturalistic and fairly detailed. Stylistically, the Birger figurine exhibits characteristics similar to bauxite carvings found at Spiro, a later Mississippian site in Oklahoma where a number of highly realistic portrayals of warriors, athletes, and priests or shamans have been found. These figures are usually dressed in specific costumes and are portrayed engaged in specific deeds, and they may represent either figures drawn from mythology or actual humans acting out the roles of mythic beings.

The reason for an association between crop cultivation and a mythological female has recently been given archaeological documentation. According to David Thomas in *Native Americans,* archaeologists have recently found evidence that plant cultivation originated independently in eastern North America sometime prior to 2000 B.C. Furthermore,

> Geneticists tell us that plants grow best in disturbed soil such as the pits, mounds, and middens surrounding Indian campsites; these became home to the weedy species, which turned into America's earliest cultivated and domesticated foods.
>
> But who was the first actually to disturb the soil and introduce seeds into it? Who was America's first geneticist? America's first farmer?
>
> Many will be surprised to learn that—accidentally or deliberately—it was the hand of woman that first domesticated the plants of the Eastern Woodlands. Throughout native America, it was always the woman who retained the botanical information. She knew exactly what plants to feed her family. She knew what plants made the best clothing and dyes, and when to harvest materials for making cordage and weaving textiles. She knew which leaves, bark, roots, stems, and berries could cure disease.
>
> And through the centuries to come, it would be the woman who would plant the seeds, tend the garden, harvest the bounty, and prepare the meal. Because she enjoyed a corner on botanical knowledge, she was the one to harness the potential of domesticated plants. For the next hundred generations, she would support thousands of people every year.
>
> Why did she do it? Did she realize the significance of her contributions to those who would follow? Was she curious, or simply anxious to experiment in order to meet the immediate needs of family and kin? Or was there some religious significance attached to providing bounty from the earth? We may never know the whole answer. (Thomas 1993, 82)

One example of corn mythology can be found among the historic Cherokee who, like most of the southern Indians in the late precontact period, were farmers. Corn was the staff of life to the Cherokee and was the subject of extensive myth and ritual. At every stage of its cultivation and harvesting, ceremonies and magical rites were performed to ensure its welfare. Thomas Lewis, a specialist on the Native Americans of Tennessee, wrote, "The common name for corn [among the Cherokee] was *tsalu,* but the name for the spirit of corn was *Agawela,* which meant 'Old Woman.' The latter name came from the Cherokee legend about the origin of corn from the body of a woman" (Lewis and Kneberg 1958, 160). Also, in a Creek myth, Corn Mother makes a special crown of knotted snakes and blue-jay feathers for her hero-son, thus indicating a mythic association between the serpent and the corn-giver.

A third female statue from southern Illinois, the Schild pipe, also depicts a kneeling woman. In her right hand she holds what appears to be a gourd.

Behind her is a large bowl, and around the base of the bowl is coiled a serpent. This figure is also carved from bauxite but, unlike the Birger and Keller figurines, has been drilled to be used as a pipe.

One of the most evocative examples of Mississippian artistry from the Cahokia area is a ceramic effigy bottle depicting a woman holding a child (see figure 16). The vessel is hollow and was probably used to carry water in a ritual context. Throughout the world, containers have traditionally been associated with women's activities, and numerous water bottles featuring depictions of women have been found in Mississippian sites. In the Cahokia example, the woman's serene expression and the tender manner in which she cradles her child attest to the artist's ability to express emotion without sacrificing formal excellence. Although this is a functional ceramic jar, it is also a sculpture, and the conveyor of a powerful set of emotions that are at once primitive and sophisticated, universal, and specific.

16. Nursing mother–effigy, ceramic, Cahokia area, St. Claire County, Illinois; Mississippian period, A.D. 1200–1400. From the collections of the St. Louis Science Center, St. Louis, Missouri.

While images of children are rare in Mississippian art, a small ceramic piece found at a site near Nashville, Tennessee, represents a baby strapped to a cradleboard (see figure 17). Mississippian graves bear grim reminders of the perils of childbirth in those times, for numerous sites contain the remains of babies and small children. Not infrequently, a young mother and her baby are found buried together. A few strands of beads and some ceramic pots were often interred with them.

17. Child on a cradleboard, ceramic, Nashville area, Tennessee; Mississippian period, A.D. 1200–1400. Courtesy of the Tennessee State Museum, Gates P. Thurston Collection of Vanderbilt University, Nashville.

Another series of female images, with examples found throughout the heartland region, depict a hunchback (see figure 18). While a few male hunchbacks have been discovered, the majority of these representations are of women, especially elderly women. Scientists have long regarded these figures as evidence of a type of tuberculosis which can have a debilitating effect on the vertebrae, but why this motif was so popular among the Mississippians remains a mystery. Perhaps its representation was a symbolic means of warding off the disease. On the other hand, such a character may have figured in the mythology of the Mississippian people. Although no myths from the historic period to support this idea have been found, it is true that among many traditional cultures deformity has often been associated with sacredness.

It is also interesting to compare the hunchbacked woman water vessels of the Southeast with the humpbacked flute player of the southwestern Anasazi. The flute player has long been recognized among southwestern Native Americans as a symbol of fertility and regeneration who carried in his hump the seeds that would replenish the barren fields. Perhaps the hunchbacked woman was a cultural heroine or a founding ancestor who also represented, in some way, the life-giving blessings of water and fertility.

Representations of specific, natural animals, while not as common as in the Woodland period, are still found in Mississippian times and may have played a role in popular mythology or acted as guardian figures or as emblems of clan-family affiliation. Especially prominent are water creatures—fish, lizards, and frogs—which may have been associated with the Underworld in general and with fertility in particular. An intriguing example, the rattler frog-effigy pipe, was discovered in a mound near Cahokia (see figure 19).

The rattler frog differs from other frog effigies in several ways; it is the only one of its type made from bauxite, and it is quite realistically portrayed. The squatting frog is depicted holding a strange bulbous object in its right "hand." While the exact nature of the object is open to speculation, it may represent a gourd rattle festooned with streamers. Similar rattler pipes were found at Spiro, but they depict humans, not frogs. Perhaps more to the point is a frog effigy found in Louisiana, also made of bauxite, which shows a large male frog holding down a female frog and squeezing eggs from the female's egg sac with his right foot. If indeed the Cahokia frog is holding a gourd and the streamers

18. Ceramic-effigy figure, Nodena Mound, Mississippi County, Arkansas. Courtesy of the University of Arkansas, Fayetteville. Photo by Zena Pearlstone.

19. Rattler frog–effigy, bauxite, East St. Louis, Illinois; Cahokia culture, Mississippian period, A.D.1000–1300. Courtesy of the Illinois State Museum, Springfield.

can be interpreted as representing rain, its associations with water and fertility are obvious. The frog, after all, figures prominently in historic southeastern Indian myths, and is frequently associated with the act of creation, the harbinger of water and of life.

A number of other frog effigies have been found in the Cahokia area. They were carved from limestone or sandstone, and all were drilled for use as pipes. Together, they represent the continuation of a long-standing tradition of frog sculptures that can be traced back to the Early Woodland period.

Many works of Mississippian art may have been inspired by the inherent tension between a popular belief system, grounded in fertility and animism, and the rapidly developing ancestor cult of the aristocracy. Between these two poles emerged the military cults, which provided a social bridge between the honors and privileges of the elite and the masses of rank-and-file farmers. Military achievement (and its twin, athletic skill) may well have been a means of social advancement among the general populace. The honored warrior was a hero to the community, someone worthy of emulation and acclaim, and images of warriors appear frequently in Mississippian art.

At the Guy Smith farm above the Big Muddy River in Jackson County, Illinois, a bauxite effigy pipe was found during the 1931 excavations led by A. R. Kelly of the University of Illinois Department of Anthropology (see figure 20).

20. Guy Smith pipe,
bauxite, Cahokia culture;
Mississippian period, A.D.
1000–1300. Courtesy of
the Museum of Natural
History, University of
Illinois, Champaign-
Urbana.

The pipe depicts a crouching warrior holding a rectangular shield. The warrior's head is turned to the right so that he peers over the shield in a posture that suggests imminent action. The implied tension is further heightened by the warrior's extended left arm, which ends in a clenched fist. The piece is extremely well modeled and highly polished, and exhibits a smoothness and roundness of form, a sensuous fullness, that brings the figure to life. Great attention was given to the face with its well-formed nose and carefully rendered eyes and ears, and the hair is shown pulled together at the top of the head in a sort of ponytail and secured with a narrow band.

Another intriguing carving from the Cahokia area is the Piasa Creek pipe, found by William McAdams in 1860 in a small mound on Piasa Creek twenty miles northwest of Cahokia. This figure is also carved from bauxite and represents a kneeling man holding what is most likely a rattle. The tubular "tie" that is shown hanging around the man's neck has been interpreted by some as a snake skin, which could suggest some association with religious activity. Again, a great deal of attention was lavished on the face and head, with an emphasis on costume details. The figure wears an animal skin headband with the tail and hind legs of the skin over his left shoulder. He appears to be wearing a helmet or bun-shaped headdress and feather-shaped earrings. The handling of the face is similar to that of the Birger figurine with its prominent nose, almond-shaped eyes, and smooth forehead. It is tantalizing to speculate on the meaning of the statue. Does the figure represent a shaman? A mythological hero? Is the rattler frog a depiction of the same mythic character in an animal guise?

Several other carvings from southern Illinois depict a seated male figure with hands resting on knees. This position seems to be conventional throughout the region, and examples of the seated figure with the legs either crossed in a lotus position or with one knee raised in a manner similar to the Chinese position of royal ease are abundant. They may represent mythic ancestors, or perhaps they are actual portraits of deceased individuals, for in many pieces the details of the face are specific.

A case in point is the Kincaid figurine discovered in 1937 (see figure 21). This statue is made of sandstone, and, once again, great attention has been given to details of the face and hair. The face, though simplified, features a sharp, aquiline nose, thin lips, and prominent ears. Vertical lines delineate the shape of the cheeks and the artist has even indicated "bags" under the almond-shaped eyes. The hair, or perhaps a headdress, is carefully executed to show a small topknot or bun and a braided or looped roll on the back of the head. An antler or wing-like form covers the right side of the head, and a broad sash or band is looped across the shoulder. A flat rectangular object, perhaps backrest or shield, is on the back of the figure.

21. Kincaid figurine,
Kincaid site, Illinois;
Mississippian period,
A.D. 1000–1300. Courtesy
of the Illinois State
Museum, Springfield.

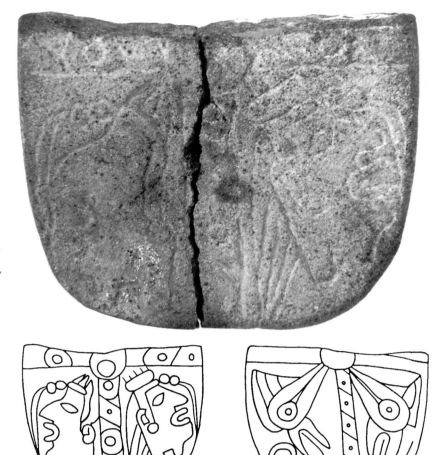

22. Ramey tablet, Monks Mound, Cahokia site, Madison County, Illinois; Cahokia culture, Mississippian period, A.D. 1000–1300. Courtesy of the Madison County Historical Society.

front　　　　　　　　　*reverse*

    In the latter part of the nineteenth century, Thomas Ramey found a small, engraved sandstone plaque in a field adjacent to Monks Mound (see figure 22). The Ramey tablet is not large—only about two inches wide—and is broken along the top edge, but it is engraved on both sides with images that provide insight into the Mississippian way of life. On the left side of the tablet, two male heads are shown in profile facing away from each other. The heads are separated by a pole decorated with circles and diagonal bands, and topped with a larger circle. Two bands extend outward from the circle at the top of the tablet to form a T. Although the heads appear at first glance to be similar, on closer examination they differ considerably. Both have serrated necks, which would seem to indicate that they depict severed heads.

The severed head is a popular motif in Mississippian art and has been interpreted as representing either an actual trophy of war or a rattle depicting a decapitated head. Decapitation of the enemy and the display of severed heads atop poles were practiced by some southeastern Indians up to postcontact times, and many Mississippian engravings show costumed warriors dancing with a war club in one hand and a severed head in the other. There is evidence at several sites in Illinois that ritual decapitation was practiced, and skeletons lacking heads were recovered from Mound 72, the burial mound of Cahokia's Great Chief. Many historians have concluded that the Mississippian people were extremely warlike and that they routinely engaged in vicious atrocities against their enemies. Spanish accounts, and those of other European explorers, tend to emphasize the brutality of the southeastern Indians, but this may be a reflection of their own bellicose intentions.

Alternatively, it has been suggested that the so-called trophy heads depicted in Mississippian art may represent the honored dead rather than the hapless victims of war. We know that Mississippian funerary practices focused on certain parts of the body—especially the head, hands, and legs—and that at many Mississippian sites the separation of the body into differently treated parts was a frequent ritual procedure. It is possible, then, that the severed heads represent, at least in some instances, the remains of the honored dead preserved for ritual treatment.

In any event, the heads on the Ramey tablet differ in subtle but important ways. They are individualized, and so apparently represent either specific individuals or mythic figures with specific physical attributes. The profile on the left has a sharp, beak-like nose, a vertical forehead, and a protruding chin, while the one on the right has a straight chin and an aquiline nose. The ears are also handled differently—only the right head wears earplugs—and the hairstyles are different. Clearly, the artist intended to depict two different people, and was careful to make these distinctions apparent.

However, rather than depicting specific individuals, the artist may be focusing on special attributes in order to identify mythic characters or clan affiliations. Just as the medieval Christian could identify certain saints by the details of their costumes or the particular types of flowers they held in their hands, the Mississippian Indians may have been able to differentiate between a number of supernatural beings on the basis of certain iconographic details.

The reverse side of the tablet has the same general format, with a band dividing the two halves and running along the top, but the heads represented are those of the ivory-billed woodpecker. Along with falcons, eagles, and other raptorial birds, the woodpecker was a frequent subject of the Mississippian artist and is often found symbolically associated with leadership and warfare. In the case of the Ramey tablet there is some ambiguity in the reading of the images, for the bird heads can be viewed as either pointing up or pointing down. In the one case, the beaks are closed and touch the circle at the top of the tablet, while the apparently severed necks hang down, trailing a line that might represent blood. Read the other way, the bird heads grow out of the circular disk and the beaks are open. Perhaps the trailing line might then be interpreted as representing sound.

A second stone tablet recovered from Cahokia shows the head and torso of a man wearing a bird costume and is thus named the bird-man tablet (see figure 23). The figure has a prominent hooked nose, a fancy headdress, earspools, a banded choker necklace, and an oval-shaped gorget on its chest. Its outstretched wing is simplified to the point of abstraction. The back of the tablet is engraved in a diamond pattern, perhaps representing feathers or scales. This piece allegedly dates from around A.D. 1300, toward the end of Cahokia's period of prominence, which may account for the stylistic difference between this work and earlier warrior representations. Although there is currently some debate regarding the authenticity of this piece, the subject of the bird-man, or falcon-impersonator, is of major significance in the history of Mississippian art and its presence at Cahokia would not be surprising.

The theme of the dancing warrior and the bird-man appears in several other areas of southern Illinois. A repoussé copper plaque representing two dancing figures was discovered at a site 100 miles south of Cahokia (see plate 9). The work dates between A.D. 1100 and 1250, corresponding to Cahokia's peak of power, and is a fine example of the repoussé technique, in which an image or design is formed in relief by working the metal from the back. The dancers wear elaborate headgear with beaded forelocks and earspools, and both carry broken maces, or war clubs, decorated with tassels. They appear to be bound together by a large vertical band that descends from above and catches them about the waist. Both dancers have turned toward the band and raise their arms as though in surprise or fear. The broken war clubs seem to echo the dancer's impotence in the face of the supernatural stream of energy from above.

Raptorial birds—or birds of prey—were a favorite subject of Mississippian artists and were almost certainly associated with mythical-religious concepts. The peregrine falcon was an especially popular subject, appearing on numerous artifacts as itself and in a number of guises, more often combined with human attributes implying a human wearing a falcon costume. Because of its speed and aggressiveness, the falcon has often been construed as a symbol of military prowess. A set of eight copper plates recovered from a grave site near St. Louis illustrate a series of man-falcon transformations (see figure 24). Some of the plates feature definite human characteristics, and others are totally avian.

Copper was more than an economic or political status symbol among

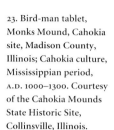

23. Bird-man tablet, Monks Mound, Cahokia site, Madison County, Illinois; Cahokia culture, Mississippian period, A.D. 1000–1300. Courtesy of the Cahokia Mounds State Historic Site, Collinsville, Illinois.

24. Wulfing plate, repoussé plaque, copper, Malden, Dunklin County, Missouri; Mississippian period, A.D. 1200–1400. By permission of Washington University Gallery of Art, St. Louis, Missouri; gift of J. Max Wulfing, 1937.

southeastern people. Its unique properties suggested mythical associations. It begins as nuggets that look like stones or pebbles, yet because of its elasticity it can be molded into flat sheets that can be cut into two-dimensional shapes. It is manipulated using fire and water—two opposing elements. Furthermore, it is transformed over time: it is at first bright gold in color, like the sun; later, especially after being buried or otherwise coming into contact with the earth, it turns blue or green. Even then, sand (earth) will clean it and it will once again shine like the sun. Because of these seemingly magical properties, copper served as a validation of spiritual power, the source of which resided with supernatural beings who controlled the primary forces and elements of nature. This power could be used either positively or negatively, and its possessions and use were limited to those whose knowledge and training would enable them to control the power resident in copper and to channel it in directions that would benefit the community.

According to art historian Amelia Trevelyan, copper ownership in the Southeast was probably hereditary (Trevelyan 1989, 63). A kinship group was entrusted by tradition with the care and ceremonial display of copper. Apparently, the only means by which one not born into copper stewardship could possess it was through deeds of extraordinary value to the community—thus the presence of copper artifacts in high-status graves and temple areas.

If the symbols of the serpent and the falcon represent, respectively, the concepts of fertility and war, the skull may be suggested as representing the cult of the ancestors in Mississippian art. While the ancient religion of fertility, regeneration, and renewal was available to everyone, the cult of the warrior was likely to have been more selective, open only to those who had the skill and energy to gain entry through their achievements. The ancestor cult was even narrower, accessible only to those who were born into it. Archaeologist James Brown wrote,

> From a political perspective, the most important formally constituted cult in southeastern societies was that organized around the veneration of the ancestors of the elite. . . . Each item deposited in the [ancestor] shrine . . . could readily be used for political purposes. The fetishes and ancestral bones represented the ultimate sacred relics. The coppers, pearls, and other sumptuary objects were tools for economic development and the means of making foreign alliances. Armaments held the potential for coercive action. These shrines assumed considerable importance in the social, economic, ritual and political life of the community. They were treated in the early historic period with notable respect and fear inspired by the powerful supernatural forces that resided with the illustrious dead (Brown 1985, 104).

One of the most obvious symbols of chiefly status was the main mode of chiefly transportation, the litter. It was a square platform suspended on a framework of four poles and was specific to the office of the central political leader throughout the Southeast. French explorers described the use of the litter among the historic Natchez of southern Mississippi. Their drawings depict the Natchez chief, Great Sun, being carried on a litter by eight bearers. We know that this tradition goes back at least to A.D. 1100 because a litter was found in Mound 72 at Cahokia in conjunction with the burial of the Great Chief there. The cross-in-circle design so frequently utilized by Mississippian artists may convey, among other meanings, the solar deity as embodied in the chief and may symbolize both the four corners of the world and the litter on which the Great Sun was borne. Other symbols of chiefly power, such as the woodpecker, are often found associated with the litter motif.

The hand-eye motif, which also appears frequently throughout the Southeast, is likely associated with chiefly power as well. The hands of the honored dead were sometimes detached from the corpse and buried separately from the rest of the body. The eye, which is often represented in the palm of the hand, may symbolize the sun, since southeastern mythology frequently describes the sun as "a blazing eye" (Brown 1985, 178). The identification of the chief with the sun was apparently widespread throughout the Southeast, and the hand-eye motif may depict a relic of the chief containing great supernatural power.

Cahokia, as one of the earliest and largest of the full-fledged Mississippian ceremonial centers, set a standard of style and grandeur against which all others can be measured. It was also one of the first to decline. The reasons for Cahokia's demise remain unresolved, although many explanations have been offered. The fact is that after two spectacular centuries—from A.D. 1100 to 1300—Cahokia began a slow slide into oblivion. There was a gradual decrease in the number of residences and the amount of pottery, not just in Cahokia but throughout the American Bottoms. Within a century the great metropolis had shrunk from a city of 40,000 residents to a town of 4,000, and by the time French explorers reached the area 300 years later there was nothing left but a few overgrown mounds. Why was the city abandoned? What prompted the people to leave this fertile land and scatter throughout the southeastern region? There is little evidence available to help us find an answer.

Despite the fortifications that went up around Cahokia in the mid-thirteenth century, there is no evidence of large-scale massacres or invasions. Was there a civil war brought on by overpopulation or disenchantment with authoritarian rule? Did agricultural problems—perhaps a loss of topsoil combined with climate changes—contribute to the migrations?

There is some evidence to support a case for agricultural problems, for between A.D. 1150 and 1350 a definite shift in climate patterns resulted in an era of warmer, wetter winters and cooler, dryer summers. A cool, dry summer is not the most conducive to growing corn, and studies of climate history have determined that the more westerly regions of the Mississippi Valley were hit hardest by the shift. A similar phenomenon was taking place at about the same time among the Anasazi of the southwestern United States, who also began to abandon their homes in the Four Corners region toward the end of the thirteenth century. There, also, there was not a mass exodus, but one by one the cities and villages declined until there was no one left.

Drought may have been the reason. Studies show that a severe drought gripped the entire region during the last quarter of the thirteenth century, a devastating blow for a people who relied on agriculture for their survival. But drought alone would probably not have driven the Anasazi from their homes. There is also evidence in the Southwest of increased fortifications during the same period, but in this case there was a clear threat from the nomadic Athabaskan people, the hunting and gathering tribes of the Great Basin, who were roving into the Four Corners region during this time. Although these small nomadic bands could not have successfully invaded and conquered fortified Anasazi towns, they could have wreaked havoc with agricultural production. Perhaps something similar happened at Cahokia.

One other possibility that has not been thoroughly investigated is the potential for serious seismic activity in the area of southern Illinois. Cahokia sits on one of the great stratigraphic faults of North America, and in the winter of 1811–12 a series of tremors that were among the most fearsome ever documented in North America shook southeastern Missouri and northern Arkansas. At New Madrid, Missouri, 150 miles south of Cahokia, residents reported eerie flashes of light, geysers of sand, and giant fissures so broad that no horse could jump them. Two additional quakes struck during the next few months, one so powerful that it rattled windows in Washington, D.C., and set church bells tolling in Richmond, Virginia. In nearby Kentucky, naturalist John James Audubon reported that "the ground rose and fell in successive furrows like the ruffled water of a lake and the earth waved like a field of corn before a breeze" (Walker 1980, 113). Although there is no evidence of sudden widespread destruction at Cahokia, even a modest series of earthquakes would have been enough to convince a concerned populace that something was terribly wrong. Combined with climate shifts and social unrest, any seismic instability might have been enough to push people over the edge, causing them to abandon their ancestral homeland in hopes of finding a safer refuge elsewhere.

The decline was a fairly local phenomenon, however, involving the American Bottoms region but not the Mississippian culture it represented. In fact, towns and trading centers with mounds, plazas, and pottery similar to those at

Cahokia began to appear elsewhere in the Southeast at about this time. Traces of new Mississippian communities have been discovered near river confluences in Tennessee, Mississippi, Georgia, West Virginia, Kansas, and Missouri.

Cahokia may never have been the capital of an empire, as has been previously suggested, but through its trade network and its advanced agricultural and architectural knowledge it did have a profound influence on the spread of Mississippian culture throughout the Southeast. It was the earliest, the largest, and the most complex of the Mississippian cities, and the development of similar ceremonial centers throughout the Southeast may have been based, at least in part, on its grand plan of public works and symbolic structures.

CHAPTER 3

The Warriors of Spiro

Ha yi! Listen!
Now instantly we have lifted up the red war club.
Quickly his soul shall be without motion
There under the earth, where the black war clubs
Shall be moving about like ball sticks in the game,
There his soul shall be, never to reappear.
We cause it to be so.
There under the earth the black war club
And the black fog have come together
As one for their covering.
The black fog shall never be lifted from them.
We cause it to be so.

"For Those About to be Slain"
Sacred Formulas of the Cherokees

ALVIN TOFFLER, in a magazine article titled "War, Wealth, and a New Era in History," wrote, "Ten thousand years ago the agricultural revolution launched the first great wave of change in human history. It led to permanent settlements and many other social and political innovations. Among the most important was war itself. Agriculture became the womb of war for two reasons. It enabled communities to produce and store economic surplus. And it hastened the development of the state" (Toffler 1991, 46).

Toffler goes on to say that while violent battles certainly occurred among preagricultural people as small groups fought to avenge killings or to gain access to hunting grounds, human conflict took on the character of war—as we understand it—only after the institution of the state had become common and after there was an economic surplus worth fighting for.

Philosopher Morris Berman, in an interview, suggested that organized warfare may have come about as a result of the Neolithic revolution, which saw the development of agriculture and the domestication of animals. What Berman calls the Self/Other split resulted in an "us/them" mentality, a system of binary thinking that emphasized the opposition of the forces of good and evil and the division of human/divine. "In Neolithic culture," he wrote, "God is seen at the top of the axis, and humans, at the bottom, must climb the ladder to God. Look at the architecture: pyramids or monumental temple structures, symbolic of the sharp division between the sacred and the secular. . . . In hunter-gatherer times, tendencies in the human psyche for conflict are indicated in the archaeological record—flint arrowheads embedded in skulls, for example. But war—organized conflict including the building of fortresses, which is the Self-Other made manifest in stone, the concept of the 'boundary,' the erection of city walls—all of this happened during the agricultural revolution" (Ferrell, 1991, 86).

Agriculture was relatively slow to develop in the ancient Southeast, where hunting and foraging continued as the main sources of sustenance long after the introduction of maize agriculture sometime after the first century A.D. During the Woodland period, Hopewell culture relied only marginally on

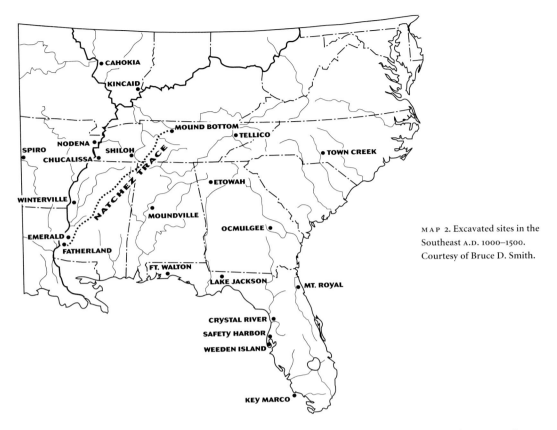

MAP 2. Excavated sites in the
Southeast A.D. 1000–1500.
Courtesy of Bruce D. Smith.

agriculture, a pattern in some parts of the Southeast up to the time of European contact in the early 1500s. Although the Hopewell people established
permanent settlements complete with large-scale public works, the bulk of
the population remained seminomadic, moving seasonally between different
camps to take advantage of a variety of ecosystems.

It is only in the late stages of the Woodland period (circa A.D. 500–900)
that the first good evidence of increased agricultural production appears. This
pattern was accompanied by significant changes in mortuary customs signaling a shift from the egalitarian structure of Hopewell society to the stratified
structure found in the Mississippian period.

"This shift," writes David Brose, "reflected a more basic change from a
ritual that rewarded or supported those who had achieved status through their
personal efforts to one that emphasized the individual who had been designated by the familial/political group to mediate between society and cosmic/
spiritual beings. . . . Late Woodland and Mississippian societies, by their adoption of an economy based on agriculture, opened themselves up to greater
ecological vulnerability. This condition could not be mitigated by developing
external social networks as long as other societies were equally vulnerable. In

situations where relationships with friends and neighbors are of little help, one naturally looks to the powers that regulate the world itself" (Brose 1985, 88–89).

Even during the Mississippian period, not all of the people living in the Southeast were farmers. Evidence from secondary mound sites in the Mississippi Valley suggests that a portion of the population, the "rural inhabitants" outside the great Mississippian centers, engaged only marginally in agriculture while continuing to rely on the ancient hunting and foraging life-style of their forebears. Even though they seem to have adopted some Mississippian innovations, such as shell-tempered pottery and certain aspects of the Southeastern Ceremonial Complex religious beliefs, they essentially remained much as they had been during the Woodland period. Their allegiance to Mississippian chiefs and their willingness to provide tribute and participate in Mississippian projects and festivals may well have been more expediency on the part of a colonized people who recognized the futility of unorganized resistance than enthusiastic acceptance of all aspects of Mississippian life. It is interesting to note just how quickly patterns of Mississippian power disappeared following the decline of the great ceremonial centers during the fifteenth and sixteenth centuries. This has been widely interpreted as resulting from a breakdown of central authority and a return to a loosely organized social structures. Perhaps for a significant portion of the population it was not so much a *return* as it was simply a continuation of social and religious patterns that had never totally disappeared during the period of Mississippian domination.

Agriculture was, however, a mainstay of the Mississippian way of life, and for those who did adopt it, which included most of the population living in or near the major ceremonial centers, the agricultural life-style carried with it a set of beliefs and customs that had an undeniable impact on the entire southeastern region.

Rich bottomland is at a premium for any agriculturalists. Rapid population growth in Mississippianized communities (due to an increased and reliable food supply) may have resulted in the development of fierce rivalries between communities in competition for access to good cropland. Each separate chiefdom may have been constantly vulnerable to attack from unfriendly neighbors, and the growing political power of Mississippian religious and military specialists may have been grounded in the general population's growing need for protection.

Farmers have usually had a hard time doubling as soldiers, especially when the time comes to plant seeds or harvest crops. They are also constantly at the mercy of the weather; even today floods, droughts, and plagues of locusts can wreak havoc in the fields. Great comfort and security would have been derived from the knowledge that skilled warriors were available to protect the village from enemy attack and that religious specialists were hard at work propitiating the powerful forces that determined the welfare of the food supply. As the importance of agriculture grew, so did the need for specialization. The development of a hierarchy of military and religious specialists is one of the major characteristics of Mississippian society.

Warriors appear to have enjoyed a great deal of status in Mississippianized communities. Recruits may have been drawn from the elite class. More probably, aspiring warriors may have advanced themselves in the hierarchy by demonstrating superior fighting skills and through acts of personal valor. They were the protectors not only of the people in the community and of the valuable food supply but also, and perhaps more important, of the chief and his family and the remains of the honored ancestors through whom the tribe could trace its history and confirm its identity.

Defensive fortifications began to appear in conjunction with Mississippian ceremonial sites in the middle of the thirteenth century. Since there is little evidence of a common external enemy, an intrusion, for example, of a large group of people from outside the Southeast, it seems likely that these fortifications appeared in response to strife within the region. As mentioned earlier, some Mississippian towns were the result of colonial intrusion on the part of the Mississippian people themselves, and the defensive structures that they built around their ceremonial centers could well have been a response to hostility on the part of the local residents. The Chickasaws, for example, who in historic times occupied the area of western Tennessee, have been described as "restless hunters who frowned on farming and the settled village life of their neighbors" (Crutchfield 1985, 48). There were no doubt many other groups throughout the Southeast who resisted the "agricultural revolution" of the Mississippians and sought to retain their own cultural identity.

Few ceremonial sites appear to have suffered large-scale attacks, however, and conventional weapons, as opposed to symbolic ones, are hardly ever found in association with the remains of those who were buried within the city's sacred center. Perhaps the defensive palisade served a symbolic as well as a mundane function by protecting the sacred inner circle of the community from supernatural as well as from natural attack. Certainly, more was at stake than just the human lives of the chief and his entourage. The sacred fire, symbolic of the life-giving warmth of the sun, and the bones of the honored dead, the very soul of the tribe, were centered within the ceremonial complex. These symbolic objects and personages had to be protected not only from enemy warriors, but also from a host of supernatural forces that constantly threatened the community's welfare. The log palisade, then, served both to deter the attack of human enemies and to demarcate the border between sacred and secular space.

The warrior appears in many guises in Mississippian art, from the naturalistic representations found in the Cahokia region to the highly conventionalized figures found on Late Mississippian shell engravings. Sometimes the warrior may represent an actual human being, as is the case with the portrait vessels from northeastern Arkansas and southeastern Missouri believed to be death portraits of warrior chiefs (Galloway 1989, 331) (see figure 25). At other times he may represent a mythological ancestor, the hero in an ancient legend. He may also represent a shaman, the warrior-priest doing battle with supernatural enemies. He is frequently pictured wearing a special costume that may include a bellows-shaped apron, a feathered cape, and an elaborate headdress with a bi-lobed arrow. He carries a war club in one hand and a severed head in the other (see figure 26). The warrior may also be represented symbolically by a creature associated with war, such as the woodpecker or, more frequently, the falcon.

James Brown identifies the falcon-impersonator as the third significant motif of chiefly iconography, the others being the chiefly litter and the chunkey player (Brown 1985, 113). The falcon-impersonator, portrayed in a broad range of styles, is represented in almost every media but most predominantly in shell and copper. The human warrior-priest, dressed in a falcon costume, is depicted dancing. Although some early historians referred to this bird-man as an "eagle dancer," a marked distinction is made in Mississippian art between the falcon and the eagle, the latter being depicted with a large beak and shaggy head feathers. Brown and others have pointed out that a number of the bird-men exhibit the forked-eye motif. It is significant that the peregrine falcon, known for its dizzying speed, its fierceness in battle, and its skill in dispatching its prey, exhibits distinctive facial markings suggesting the forked-eye motif (see figure 27).

25. Human head–effigy vessel, ceramic, Mississippi County, Arkansas; Late Mississippian period, A.D. 1300–1500. Courtesy of the University of Arkansas, Fayetteville. Photo by Zena Pearlstone.

26. Gorget with falcon-impersonator, shell; Mississippian period, A.D. 1200–1450. Courtesy of the National Museum of the American Indian, Smithsonian Institution. By permission of the National Museum of the American Indian, Smithsonian Institution, Washington, D.C. (#20815).

The chunkey player's significance in Mississippian iconography is still obscure, but the many representations of this subject imply a more than mundane interest in the images of this athlete. As in Mesoamerica, the chunkey player may have represented an ancestor, a cultural hero, or a divine athlete.

Interestingly, the attributes of the chunkey player are, in several instances, combined with those of the falcon-impersonator. In at least one example, the hand of the player resembles the talons of a bird. The player also exhibits the forked eye and may wear the bellows-shaped apron. Instead of a war club, he carries a chunkey stick. What the connection may be is open to speculation, but the similarities are intriguing. Perhaps the same mythic hero is being represented in two different roles: the warrior who protects the tribe and the athlete-diviner who could see the future in the intersection of the sun disk and the lance.

The famous big boy–effigy pipe from Spiro, Oklahoma, is a rare example of the falcon-warrior portrayed in three-dimensional form (see plate 10). This elegant bauxite sculpture depicts a costumed man seated in a cross-legged position with his hands resting on his knees. He seems poised on the edge of making a move, and his face reflects deep concentration. He wears a flat cap or disk decorated with an ogee (double curve) symbol and held in place by a strap around his head. Strings of beads hang from his neck, and his hair is pulled back into a heavy braid that falls forward over his left shoulder. He also wears a feathered cape and ear ornaments representing the Long-Nosed God.

The idea of a long-nosed hero has an extensive history in the eastern United States. Small shell maskettes depicting a long-nosed face have been found in the northern Mississippi Valley and are among the earliest artifacts associated with the Mississippian culture. During historic times the Winnebagos had as one of their culture heroes Red Horn, also known as He Who Wears Human Heads As Earrings. It has been suggested that because of his mythic association with the morning star and a variety of other solar phenomena, Red Horn may have once been one manifestation of the sun. Art historian Robert Hall has compared myths of the Winnebago hero Red Horn with those of the Mexican myth of Quetzalcoatl, who was also associated with the morning star and who was himself a long-nosed god. "The . . . Winnebago idea of a hero who had earrings in the form of human heads could easily have been part of a mythic tradition responsible for the appearance of the long-nosed god and the related short-nosed masquettes on the ears of human figures in the art of the prehistoric Spiro site in Oklahoma. . . . The stories of Red Horn . . . tie into the Mesoamerican mythology of long-nosed gods with various sun, dawn and Venus associations" (Hall in Galloway 1989, 247).

Several other attributes of the Mississippian warrior, such as the bi-lobed arrow and the severed head, are also paralleled by the attributes of Mesoamerican solar deities. In both Winnebago and Mexican myths, a hero believed to have been associated with the morning star engages in a contest with a super-

27. Peregrine falcon. From the collection of the Michigan State University Museum, East Lansing. Photo by James A. Brown.

natural enemy; he is defeated and beheaded, and his head is hung on a pole. In both cases the hero has a son by each of two wives, one a woman with red hair who belonged to the village of the supernatural enemy. The sons of the hero, in both stories, discover the head or bones of the father, recover them, and reassemble them after destroying the enemy. A ball game, in which the members of the losing team are killed or sacrificed, is also common to both myths.

Archaeologists have found no evidence of the direct intrusion of Meso-american goods or concepts into the Mississippi Valley. However, it has been suggested that while Mississippian culture was not directly related to cultural developments in Mexico, it may have represented a parallel evolution from old religious archetypes of North American origin. As Malcolm Webb put it, "Mississippian culture came to resemble Mesoamerican because, having the same stock of basic expressive forms to draw upon, it came to use them in a parallel fashion to meet similar needs that emerged as it recapitulated . . . the same social evolutionary developments leading from tribe to chiefdom to state" (Webb in Galloway 1989, 293).

A good deal of what scholars know about Mississippian religious beliefs has been based on the wealth of material recovered from the ancient Mississippian city near Spiro in eastern Oklahoma. Much of the material recovered from the site deals with warfare and warrior imagery or depicts composite beasts or supernatural beings. This may be why there has been a tendency among scholars of southeastern art and religion to emphasize the cult of the warrior (and his symbol, the falcon-impersonator) at the expense of the female-oriented belief system suggested by the Birger and Keller statues from Cahokia.

In comparison with Cahokia, Spiro is a modest mound group and village covering about eighty acres, although the extended edges of the site may cover an additional fifty acres (see figure 28). There were originally nine mounds in the town, only three of which were platform mounds. The mounds occur in two clusters, each apparently devoted to specialized activities. Six of the mounds comprise a western group, which may have included an oval plaza. The eastern group has three mounds, the largest of which, the Craig Mound, is actually four conjoined mounds that may have provided the base for at least four successive flat-topped mounds on which were situated charnel houses—special buildings for the preparation and disposal of the dead. The western mound group appears to have been the site of religious and political ceremonies for the living; the eastern cluster seems to have been devoted exclusively to activities surrounding the dead.

The unusual layout of the Spiro site is not the only anomaly that separates it from other Mississippian ceremonial centers. It lies at the extreme western edge of the Mississippian cultural area and may have had more in common with the Plains culture than with that of other agricultural centers east of the

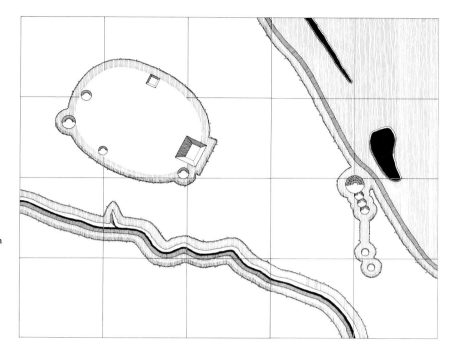

28. Spiro site, Spiro, Oklahoma; Mississippian period, A.D. 1000–1400. From *Prehistoric Architecture in the Eastern United States* by William N. Morgan (Cambridge: The MIT Press, 1980).

Mississippi. The Spiro inhabitants are thought to have been part of the Caddoan-speaking peoples who lived along the Red River, and following the abandonment of the Spiro ceremonial center around A.D. 1450 it is thought that most of the population probably moved west onto the southern plains, where they became part of the Caddoan-affiliated tribes of the Wichita or Kichai.

The site went through several phases of activity beginning in about A.D. 600, when it was used by nomadic hunters as a burial ground. By A.D. 800 there was a substantial village on the site and the beginnings of ceremonial mound construction. Between A.D. 800 and 1250, the egalitarian social structure characteristic of the Woodland culture was replaced at Spiro by a pre-state chiefdom controlled by lineage or class. The ruling class began participating actively in an extensive pansoutheastern trade network, importing shell, copper, and other exotic goods from Mississippian centers throughout the Southeast.

By the beginning of the Spiro III Phase (A.D. 1250), no evidence of residential population is to be found within two or three miles of the mounds themselves. The mound area appears to have been designated a purely ceremonial site—a sort of little Vatican City—where only religious specialists and their associates worked and lived. This period saw an enormous increase in the importation of Mississippian trade items, and almost all of the amazing wealth of art works found in the Craig Mound were placed there during this phase. Art historian Dennis Peterson wrote, "The art found in Spiro burials was more than art; it communicated ideas and ideology about which archaeologists can only theorize. The motifs used in Spiro elite art echo those used throughout the Mississippian culture area, but the combinations of motifs in Spiro art have a diversity not seen in other . . . sites. Why Spiro leaders fostered such experiments is unknown" (Peterson in Galloway 1989, 120).

The treasure taken from the Craig Mound at Spiro is the closest thing we have in Mississippian archaeology to something like King Tut's tomb. So rich in amount and quality were the Spiro treasures that they almost single-handedly reshaped archaeological understanding of the Indian cultures of the Southeast and formed the basis for the concept of the Southern Cult, a pansoutheastern set of religious beliefs and practices more recently referred to as the Southeastern Ceremonial Complex. The thousands of engraved shell cups and gorgets recovered from the site provided scientists and art historians with a major body of Mississippian work to examine and analyze. Themes, motifs, and symbols could be identified and compared, stylistic groupings suggested, and chronological development observed. "What are we to make of the engraved shells from Spiro?" wrote Jeffrey Brain in *Archaeology Magazine.*

> Dramatically, the artwork treats of spiritual and ceremonial matters, of death and sacrifice. There are composite beings, for example—supernatural figures blending human and animal elements. There are human figures impersonating animals, and people clothed in regalia of more abstract significance. There are weapons, often broken ones, corpses and severed heads. Most of the animals depicted, whether in whole or in part, are predatory creatures—raptorial birds, rattlesnakes and felines. Some of the activities suggested are obscure in their meaning, but they too, like so much of the decoration, seem somehow sinister. It is clearly a man's world; there is no intimation of procreation or of domestic pursuits. The designs seem strange and frightening, perhaps because we do not understand their significance or function. (Brain 1988, 25)

Yet, Spiro remains an atypical site in so many ways that it is difficult to trust a view of Mississippian art and religion based on the Spiro example. What has become clear is that the Spiro elite were active collectors of exotic artifacts that they apparently acquired through trade with other Mississippians from the Great Lakes to the Gulf Coast. A large number of copper artifacts were taken from the Craig site, yet metalworking workshops are unknown at Spiro, and good sources of native copper are more than 300 miles away. Furthermore, stylistic analysis of the Spiro shell cups indicates that nearly 700 different artists did the engraving; only rarely did the same artist decorate more than two cups. Either the cups were engraved at a number of sites and transported to Spiro, or a considerable percentage of the Spiro population was engaged in decorating cups. Wrote James Brown, "The single-source argument for both the engraved shell and copper repoussé plates rests only on the quantitative concentration of these materials at Spiro. This argument offers as many problems as solutions. But thinking of the distribution of these materials as part of a larger style distribution problem opens up an alternative perspective that places craft production in locations other than Spiro" (Brown in Galloway 1989, 188).

Just as the Birger and Keller statues found at Cahokia were likely produced in Arkansas and transported to the Illinois ceremonial center, so many, if not most, of the artifacts included in the Spiro treasure trove likely came from a variety of locations over a period of many years. Perhaps specific towns specialized in the production of exotic religious paraphernalia. Maybe even certain families held the "rights" to the portrayal of certain subjects, much as the carving families of the Northwest coast owned, and still own, access to specific myths and images. Despite its amazing wealth of artistic treasures, Spiro remains a mystery; it poses more questions than it answers.

What does seem clear is that the Spiro elite had a marked preference for artwork that glorified the warrior and dealt with themes of war and sacrifice. The themes of fertility and procreation, of Corn Mothers and cultivators, are largely absent from the Spiro repertoire. In many other Mississippian sites, depictions of warriors, winged serpents, and severed heads are tempered by the presence of images of women, children, and naturalistic animals, but at Spiro, unless we have misinterpreted the content of these remarkable works of art, images of destruction and death hold sway. Were the early Oklahomans the Spartans of Mississippian society—a warrior race interested only in the glory of battle and the sweetness of revenge? Or are these sinister images symbolic of frightening supernatural forces that had to be propitiated through sacrifice and ritual?

One of the reasons for the many enigmas surrounding the Spiro site lies in the archaeological catastrophe that it suffered during the 1930s at the hands of a group of unprincipled men. Calling themselves the Pocola Mining Company and inspired by the unusual artifacts that had so far been recovered from the site, this group of grave robbers launched a commercial venture aimed at unearthing and selling the "Indian curiosities" in hopes of making a tremendous profit. They secured a lease on the property and began digging up the largest mound—the Craig Mound. What they found was a mortuary deposit of unprecedented proportions—the largest by far ever found in the Southeast. Thousands of objects were looted from the site with no regard for their associations or context. Many of the pieces were purposefully broken so that the pieces could be sold separately. Collectors, curiosity-seekers, and a handful of local archaeologists came to the site and joined in buying the grave goods, which were sold at the mouth of the tunnel leading to the mound. Some entrepreneurs even set up shop and grabbed up artifacts as soon as they were brought out (Brain 1988, 21).

Opposition to the looting increased, and in the spring of 1935 the Oklahoma state legislature passed an antiquities act, one of the earliest state statutes aimed at regulating archaeological excavations. In 1936 the Works Project Administration, with the cooperation of the University of Oklahoma and the Oklahoma Historical Society, launched a program to excavate scientifically what was left of the Craig Mound, along with other important features of the site.

Today, Spiro Mounds Archaeological State Park, leased from the Army Corps of Engineers, preserves what remains of one of the most interesting and important Mississippian sites in the Southeast. The reconstructed Craig and Ward mounds, along with a typical thatch-roofed house, give the visitor some idea of the dimensions of the original town. Most of the artifacts excavated since the 1935 looting have gone into public collections in Oklahoma and elsewhere. The losses to archaeology, and to the world, fostered by the Pocola Mining Company were enormous, but many of the original artifacts found homes in private collections that eventually came into the public domain, including one that was given to the Smithsonian Institution's United States National Museum. Through access to museum collections, archaeologists and art historians have been able to gain a great deal of additional knowledge about the site and the people who lived in the area. This knowledge may eventually enable us to reconstruct the lost heritage of Spiro.

The problem of cultural erosion is certainly not confined to any one time or place. The Spiro disaster brought the issue of site destruction to an early head in Oklahoma, resulting in legislation aimed at reducing the damage to historically significant sites rendered by amateurs and looters. Other states have not necessarily followed suit. For example, until 1991 there were no laws in Oklahoma's next-door neighbor, Arkansas, to protect artifacts in unmarked burial sites on private property, nor were there any prohibitions against the sale or the transfer of these artifacts across state lines. The result has been the widescale destruction of many important Mississippian sites, especially in the northeastern part of the state.

It is in this region that many of the spectacular ceramic "head pots" were produced (see figure 25). These effigy-head vessels with slit-like eyes and grimacing mouths may be the death masks of deceased warriors, perhaps intended to hold the cremated remains of the honored dead. The vessels are quite distinctive and often include decorations depicting tattooing or scarification. Some of the subjects appear to be youthful, others are old.

The Mississippians of Arkansas had a strong tradition of mortuary sculpture, including human figurines that may have represented founding ancestors. Some of these statues are also quite specific in detail, indicating special face and body painting or tattooing. Most of these vessels date from the protohistoric period (circa A.D. 1550–1650), and they have become quite popular with collectors as the market for Native American art has escalated.

The rapid appreciation of American Indian art, whether ancient or modern, has led to grave-robbing activities nationwide. In an article titled "The Looting of Arkansas" in *Archaeology Magazine*, Spencer Harrington wrote, "The conflict between archaeologists and collectors is by no means exclusive to Arkansas. It is symptomatic of a country that by and large has failed to define its national heritage or how to preserve it, a situation that has led to a spectacular amount of site destruction, a vanishing data base for scientists, and acts of gross insensitivity toward Native Americans" (Harrington 1991, 24).

In most of the world, cultural treasures are nationalized. Imagine the problems that would be encountered in trying to dig up a fifth-century Greek statue and transport it out of Greece! Yet in the United States, property owners have continued to determine not only the fate of archaeologically significant sites on their land but also the fate of artifacts taken from those sites. Harrington wrote, "Is it 'looting' to dig up a grave on your own property (or with permission, on someone else's) and keep or sell the burial artifacts? In about half the states in this country the answer is no" (Harrington 1991, 24).

Our historical perspective has been further perverted by the persistence of the notion that American history began in 1492. This misconception is being slowly erased, but much important material from precontact times has already been lost and more is lost every day. The Native American Grave Protection and Repatriation Act, signed by President George Bush in November 1990, allows Native American groups the right to reclaim identifiable human remains and associated burial artifacts from museums that receive federal support. In compliance with that law, a number of museums have already undertaken an inventory of their collections and have notified appropriate tribes of the results. The tribes can then make claims on objects of ceremonial significance. The new law also grants to Native Americans legal claim on all human remains and grave goods excavated on federal lands, but it does not apply to those found on state or private property.

The issue is far from settled. Collectors, museum professionals, archaeologists, art historians, and American Indians will continue an uneasy dance as they struggle to resolve this many-sided problem. "The fate of this country's cultural resources," wrote Harrington, "is ultimately not only an archaeological question or a question of property owner's rights, but also an issue of how we will choose to perceive ourselves and our past" (Harrington 1991, 30).

CHAPTER 4

The Sacred Sites of Western Tennessee

SOME THREE HUNDRED miles to the south of Cahokia lies the modern city of Memphis, Tennessee, and in the southern suburbs, now part of the T. O. Fuller State Park, is the Mississippian city of Chucalissa. Chucalissa is a Choctaw Indian word meaning "abandoned house," and this ceremonial center was abandoned around A.D. 1500 after approximately 500 years of occupation. The mound complex is located on a bluff overlooking the rich bottomland of the Mississippi River, which can be glimpsed in the distance. Remnants of a palisade form an arc around the eastern perimeter of the complex while the bluff provides a natural fortification to the west (see figure 29). It is estimated that at its height (between A.D. 1200 and 1400), approximately 1,000 people lived in the immediate area—a fair-sized town by Mississippian standards.

Chucalissa has been extensively reconstructed by archaeologists from Memphis State University to depict daily life in the precontact village. An indoor museum displays material recovered from the site along with artifacts from other sites in the area. Choctaw Indians act as guides and demonstrate traditional crafts on the Chucalissa grounds. An annual Choctaw pow-wow is held in August with stickball games, dancing, and ceremonies.

While some might question the full authenticity of the Chucalissa reconstruction, those responsible have attempted to "put flesh on the bones" of the precontact inhabitants. Based on the accounts of two French explorers, Charlevoix and De Montigny, who, among others, visited the Southeast around 1700, Memphis State archaeologists have constructed thatch-roofed structures atop the principal mounds (see figures 30 and 31) and installed dioramas to interpret various aspects of Mississippian culture. For example, inside the chief's house a peace ceremony is in progress.

"When one tribe wished to obtain a favor of the Chief of another tribe, ambassadors would approach the Chief," wrote William Hancock, preparator at the C. H. Nash Museum, Chucalissa. "They entered the village in procession, chanting with drum and rattle. Some wore feathers in their ears and

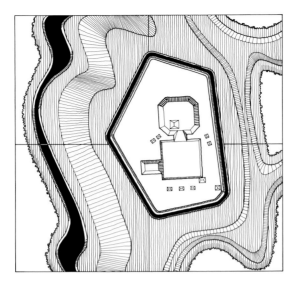

29. Chucalissa site,
Memphis, Tennessee;
Mississippian period,
A.D. 1100–1500. From
*Prehistoric Architecture
in the Eastern United
States* by William N.
Morgan (Cambridge:
The MIT Press, 1980).

hair, and painted their faces red and black. Upon entering the Chief's house, the pipe was offered. An orator spoke at length asking for a continuation of friendship, to gain assistance against an enemy, or to end hostilities between the two tribes. The Chief, surrounded by his officers and nobles in all their finery, could accept or reject the pipe, thereby granting or refusing the request" (Hancock n.d.).

Five figures are represented in the peace ceremony diorama—the chief, a master of ceremonies, an honored woman (probably the chief's sister), a war chief (traditionally the chief's younger brother), and a war captain. Costume details of the reconstructed scene are based on a variety of ethnographic accounts (and some educated guesses) and may or may not coincide exactly with those of the precontact inhabitants. However, the reconstructions provide an interesting catalog of the paraphernalia traditionally associated with the Mississippian elite and may give some insights into the function of various ritual items. For example, the chief, the master of ceremonies and the honored woman are all shown wearing feathered capes. There are a number of references to the feathered cape as part of the costume of the Mississippian nobility. Ranjel, in the de Soto narratives of 1541–43, described the chief of the Tascalusa as wearing a mantle of feathers (Bourne 1904, 120). Du Pratz, in a later account of the Natchez, mentioned that feathered capes were worn by "women of the honored class" (Swanton 1911, 63). Speaking of the Creeks, William Bartram stated that "some have a short cloak, just large enough to cover the shoulder and breast: this is most ingeniously constructed of feathers woven or placed in a most natural imbricated manner, usually of the scarlet feathers of flamingo" (Bartram 1958, 500). Fragments of feather capes have been recovered from the

Spiro site in Oklahoma and at the Etowah site in Georgia, and a feathered cape is pictured on any number of bird-man images in a variety of media from sites throughout the region. In addition, a ceramic burial urn from the Buck Mound near Fort Walton Beach, Florida, depicts a masked figure wearing a feathered cape (see plate 3). Since this piece dates from the Weeden Island period (c. A.D. 600–900), it might be assumed that the feathered cape was already established as an emblem of authority even before the development of the Mississippian hierarchy.

Another costume detail depicted at Chucalissa is the feather fan. A shell engraving from Spiro depicts a dancer carrying a feathered fan, while a copper plate depicts a dancer carrying a fan in a pocket of his apron. James Adair mentioned that "during some of the dances of the Creek Indians, men . . . carried turkey feather fans in their left hands as a sign of leadership" (Adair 1775, 423), while in Swanton's account of the southeastern Indians we find that "the proper possession of this fan is with the older men and the Chiefs who spend much of their time in leisure. They handle the fan very gracefully in emphasizing their gestures and in keeping insects away. During ceremonies, to carry a fan is a sign of leadership" (Swanton 1911, 456).

Southeastern leaders wore a variety of elaborate headdresses made of copper, feathers, antlers, and other materials. In describing a Natchez chief, du Pratz noted that "he wore a crown of white feathers mingled with red" (Swanton 1911, 144), and at the chief's funeral the master of ceremonies was "adorned with red feathers in a half-crown" (Swanton 1911, 148). Copper disks also appear on a variety of Mississippian figures as part of the headdress. A

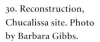

30. Reconstruction, Chucalissa site. Photo by Barbara Gibbs.

31. Thatch roof from the reconstruction, Chucalissa site. Photo by Barbara Gibbs.

copper plate from Etowah shows a figure costumed as a hawk with what appears to be a hawk plate on his forehead surrounded by a sun-like disk. Excavations at Etowah revealed that copper plates were commonly buried with the elite, being found on the foreheads of skulls. Similar plates were found in graves in Missouri. And the big boy pipe from Spiro includes a large disk as part of the figure's headgear (see plate 10).

Deer antlers were also used extensively as a costume element, and deer antler headdresses can be seen on shell and copper engravings from many different sites. A set of copper-covered deer antlers from Spiro were apparently part of a headdress. A copper-covered mask with deer antlers has also been reconstructed from material found at Etowah.

The mace and the bi-lobed arrow are two other costume elements in the Chucalissa reconstruction. Du Pratz, in his account of the Natchez, quotes an elderly warrior as asking, "How many blows of the war club have I made against my enemies in order not to be taken!" (Swanton 1911, 130). According to du Pratz, the Natchez master of ceremonies "carried a red baton in the shape of a cross at the end of which hung a cluster of black feathers" (Swanton 1911, 148). Stone maces have been found all over the Southeast. Several were painted. One was divided into red and white halves, another was red and black, and a third was painted red. Many of the dancers pictured in shell and copper engravings carry a mace in one hand and a severed head in the other. Overlooking the Mound Bottom site near Nashville, Tennessee, the image of a stone mace was found carved in a large boulder at the top of a cliff.

The bi-lobed arrow is yet another emblem found extensively throughout the Mississippian Southeast. It appears frequently in depictions of costumed dancers in the company of other elements such as the mace, bellows-shaped apron, war club, and severed head. A multitude of speculation surrounds this motif. Some scholars suggest that it represents a phallic symbol; others believe it is a stylized war club, a bow and arrow, or an atlatl. Some think that it symbolized a moon/sun, male/female duality—a suggestion of paired opposites not unlike the yin/yang symbol of Asia—while others call attention to the similarity in shape of the bi-lobed arrow and a type of hallucinogenic mushroom (Trevelyan 1989).

The Long-Nosed God also appears in the Chucalissa reconstruction in the form of ear decorations worn by the chief. According to David Brose, the ear ornaments worn by falcon-impersonators include Long-Nosed God maskettes made of marine shell or copper. "Widely distributed during the classic phase of artistic development (A.D. 1000–1300), they held symbolic associations that are obscure today, partly because this type of ear ornament passed from use by the end of that phase" (Brose 1985, 123).

Feathered capes, copper headdresses, ceremonial weapons, elaborate jewelry—these were the emblems of leadership reserved for the highest level of Mississippian society. They may have indicated spiritual as well as political authority, for in Mississippian society there was no separation of church and state. Many of the costume elements associated with the elite were probably also emblems of spiritual power and may have been "owned" by certain families whose authority was based on ancestral ties. These costume elements were probably embellished with special hairdos, tattoos, and face and body painting that further identified the lineage and ritual associations of Mississippian leaders.

The chief and his entourage must have presented an awesome spectacle as they passed through the town en route to the sacred temple mound to preside over the great ceremonies and festivals that marked the Mississippian year. Such rites had been observed for as long as anyone could remember, part of the cycle of the seasons and the great wheel of birth, death, and rebirth. Each detail of the participant's costume, each object which he or she carried, contributed to the spiritual significance of the occasion and identified the individual within the context of the sacred cosmology.

It was during the period A.D. 1000–1300 that most of the major themes of Mississippian art were firmly established in the Mississippi Valley and adjacent regions and slowly filtered southward and eastward along trade routes. Certain symbolic images, such as the hand-eye, the sun circle, and the Long-Nosed God, were elaborations on, or continuations of, motifs already established during the preceding periods. Others, such as the bi-lobed arrow, the ceremonial mace, the chunkey player, and the falcon-impersonator, were either innovations or more elaborate extensions of earlier themes. These stylistic developments appear to correspond to the rise of the Southeastern Ceremonial Complex, the loosely organized transregional "religion" that gave Mississippian culture its stylistic and ideological integrity.

Much of the art done during this period is representational, even naturalistic. In this sense, it is an extension of the representational art of the Hopewell period except that Mississippian artists dealt more extensively with human subjects. Stylistically, Brown and others suggest that this period includes works done in the Braden style of Oklahoma and the so-called Mound C style found at Etowah in northern Georgia, along with the Mississippi Valley style seen at Cahokia, Shiloh, and elsewhere in the heartland region. These works are characterized by highly detailed, faithfully scaled reproductions of real objects.

THE ORIGINS AND SIGNIFICANCE of the ball game in Mississippian society is still open to speculation. Some scholars point to the presence of ball courts in Mississippian towns as evidence of contact with Mesoamerica, yet there is no proof of a direct link with Mexico. Such is not the case with early settlements in the Southwest, where ceremonial and luxury artifacts such as copper bells, mosaic mirrors, and rubber balls were being imported directly from Mexico. At the Hohokam settlement of Snaketown, near present-day Phoenix, a ball court the size of a football field was discovered along with platform mounds, stone paint palettes, and hundreds of clay figurines.

In Mesoamerica, the ball game was a religious spectacle that went far beyond sport. The ritual ball games of the Maya and Toltec were probably based on the movements of the cosmos, and were intended to ensure the continuation of the vital forces of nature. Among the Muskhogean people of the Eastern Woodlands, a similar ball game, called "the little brother of war," may have served as an outlet for the aggressive and competitive emotions that could lead to armed confrontation. The Lakota holy man, Black Elk, described the ball game's significance among his people as follows: "There was, until recently, a game among our people which was played with a ball, four teams and four goals which were set up at the four quarters. But there are only a few of us today who still understand why the game is sacred, or what the game originally was long ago, when it was not really a game, but one of our most important rites. The game as it is played today represents the course of a man's life, which should be spent in trying to get the ball, for the ball represents Wakan-Tanka, or the universe. In the game it is very difficult to get the ball, for the odds—which represent ignorance—are against you, and it is only one or two of the teams who are able to have the ball, and if you think about what the ball represents, you will see that there is much truth in it" (Brown 1971, 127).

In the Southeast, a ball game similar to modern lacrosse was incorporated by historic tribes into the Boskita, or Busk, the great summer ceremony of propitiation and renewal that still marks the beginning of the Native American New Year (see figure 32). Whether or not the modern stickball game had its origins in a Mississippian period prototype, the archaeologist Thomas Lewis provides a colorful description of this lively event and its importance to historic period Indians:

Sides are chosen, with sixty players on each side. Their bodies are brilliantly painted, they are dressed in breech clouts and moccasins; attached to the back of the breech clouts are the tails of swift-footed animals. Each player carries two ball sticks shaped somewhat like small tennis rackets, made of hickory and strung with deer hide thongs. . . . The small ball is made of deer hair covered with deer skin and sewed with deer sinew. The field is nearly a quarter of a mile long with a goal at each end formed by two uprights and a crossbar. . . . All the players rush out and throw down their rackets. These must be counted to make sure that each side has the same number. Then the men divide into five squads, with the opposing

32. Indians playing the ball game; de Bry after Le Moyne. Courtesy of Rare Books and Manuscripts, The New York Public Library/ Astor, Lenox, and Tilden Foundations.

players facing each other along the two sides of the field. The ball is tossed into the air by an old man, and the contest is on. A player catches the ball with his rackets, and either runs with it or throws it. The objective is to hit either the goal post or crossbar with the ball. After each goal, the ball is put back in play at the center of the field. An especially good player must be wary because his opponents will deliberately try to injure him and put him out of the game. When that happens, the other side must also discard a player, but it is certain not to be one of their best. . . . Whenever a goal is made, a tally is stuck in the ground by a scorekeeper for that team. After ten goals, the sticks are withdrawn one at a time to score the subsequent points. The first side to score twenty points wins the game. Quantities of valuable objects are wagered on the outcome. . . . The winning players run to their goals and perform an exultant dance, while the other team takes to its heels. The losing group is jeered and especially derided by those who bet on them. (Lewis and Kneberg 1946, 131)

In Mesoamerica, the ball game was deeply imbued with the imagery of death and sacrifice, and the postgame ceremonies may have included the sacrifice of the losers.

A second contest still being played by the Creeks in historic times was the chunkey game. Each Creek town had a chunkey yard, a large square court scraped smooth and level. This game was played with a large disk, three to six

33. Chunkey stone, ground and polished stone, Hardin County, Kentucky; Mississippian period, A.D. 1200–1400. Collection of the Harn Museum of Art, University of Florida, Gainesville.

inches in diameter, made from fine-grained stone. Almost perfectly symmetrical and highly polished, the disks are beautiful objects in their own right (see figure 33). According to John Swanton in his *Indians of the Southeastern United States,* these stone disks were kept in the towns and were considered valuable heirlooms. The game is described by Swanton as follows: "The essence of the game was to start the stone roller along a smooth piece of ground . . . after which the two players threw their poles after it with the idea of hitting the stone, coming as near it as possible when the stone came to rest, or preventing the opponents from accomplishing either of these results" (Swanton 1946, 682).

In Mississippian art, the chunkey player is usually depicted holding a stone disk and striped sticks. In some depictions, the player's costume includes a looped belt and a distinctive spool-shaped hat. Brown believes that the chunkey player's role may have been associated originally with divination. He bases this premise on the Cherokee myth of Wild Boy who, in the course of his search for his father, uses a "gaming wheel" to determine the correct direction in which he should travel. "It is reasonable to postulate that the configuration in which a striped pole and chunkey stone landed with respect to each other would have been fruitful material for 'reading'" (Brown 1985, 112), much as the cast sticks of the I-Ching were read by the ancient Chinese.

Chunkey stones, first manufactured some time after A.D. 800, are frequently found in the graves of the Mississippian elite, along with Southeastern Ceremonial Complex symbols such as the mace and the baton. The high degree of respect shown toward the stones up to historic times may be based on their religious significance as part of the hierarchical structure of Mississippian society. A Spanish account of a chunkey game from 1595 notes that only the chief and his principal men took part (Larson 1989, 128–29). Perhaps, then, the chunkey game was part of the complex ritual and social functions reserved for the Mississippian elite.

A bauxite chunkey player–effigy from eastern Oklahoma, now in the St. Louis Museum, may represent a mythic figure, the athlete elevated to heroic stature (see plate 11). Naked except for his exotic jewelry and elaborate headdress, he carries a stone disk in his right hand and two sticks in his left. His expression is grave, his body composed, yet there is a feeling of intense concentration, of heightened anticipation, as though he is waiting for the signal to spring up and begin the game. He has about him a feeling of latent energy, the potential for motion in the moment just before the action occurs. One has only to look to the mortuary sculpture of the same region to appreciate the liveliness of the heroic style (see figure 34).

The Shiloh site in Shiloh Military Park, located some sixty miles east of Memphis, Tennessee, also has yielded a fine example of early Mississippian

34. Seated male figure,
wood, Craig Mound,
Spiro site, LeFlore
County, Oklahoma;
Caddoan culture,
Mississippian period,
A.D. 1200–1350.
Photo by Dirk Baaker,
The Detroit Institute of
Arts. On permanent loan
to the Smithsonian
Institution from the
Thomas Gilcrease
Institute of American
History and Art, Tulsa,
Oklahoma.

figurative sculpture. The park commemorates a decisive Civil War battle on April 6 and 7, 1862. Today, cannons sit mute among the rolling meadows and shady groves of the Tennessee countryside, and plaques and piles of cannonballs mark the places where the fiercest fighting occurred. Tourists wander along the trails, pausing to read the markers and study their guidebooks, musing about those fateful days in April just over a century ago when Union and Confederate troops clashed in fatal combat. Most of the visitors seem unaware that on the northeast edge of the park lie the ruins of an ancient town where other battles raged more than five hundred years before the Battle of Shiloh.

The Shiloh Mississippian site is located on a high bluff overlooking a wide curve of the Tennessee River. From the top of the main ceremonial mound, one has a spectacular view of the river some sixty feet below—a wide silver ribbon winding through dense green forests (see plates 12 and 13). Directly across the river, rich bottomlands stretch eastward toward the distant hills. One can easily imagine the grandeur of a sunrise seen from such a vantage point—copper sunbeams reflecting off the water, light flooding the horizon above the violet, mist-shrouded forest.

Looking west from the top of the mound, one can see two other large mounds directly across a wide plaza. The three large mounds are arranged in a triangular pattern that gives the seven-mound complex a unity and grace that is quite satisfying (see figures 35–37). The pyramidal mounds were constructed between A.D. 1000 and 1250. Architect William Morgan, who described the Shiloh site in the book *Prehistoric Architecture in the Eastern United States,* writes, "Shiloh's comparatively well-preserved structures have almost perfectly square bases and are more notable for their disciplined proportions than for their large sizes" (Morgan 1980, 111). And Clarence Moore, who visited the site in 1915, wrote enthusiastically about the "seven beautiful, symmetrical, aboriginal mounds" he found there (Moore 1915).

Two lines of fortifications enclose the Shiloh site. The outer wall is nearly a mile and a quarter long and has a series of bastions spaced along its length. An inner wall parallels the outer defensive earthwork. Originally, a log palisade ran along the length of both walls.

A short distance to the south of the pyramidal mound complex is an elliptical burial mound. In 1899 an archaeological party headed by Colonel Cornelius Cadle excavated the mound and found the remains of a log tomb containing a number of artifacts, including a magnificent platform pipe representing a kneeling man (see plate 14). Made of fine-grained bauxite, the Shiloh pipe is similar both technically and stylistically to other Mississippian stone effigies found at Cahokia and at other sites in the Mississippi River Valley heartland from St. Louis, Missouri, to Vicksburg, Mississippi. In fact,

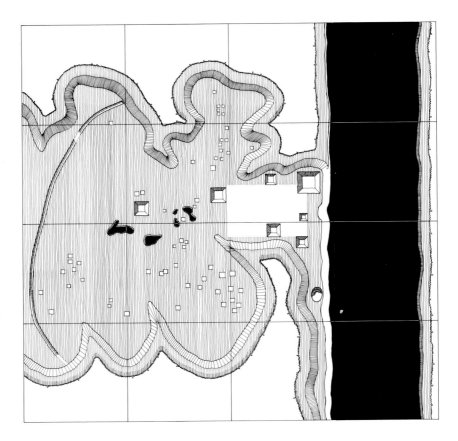

35. Shiloh site, McNairy County, Tennessee; Mississippian period, A.D. 1000–1250. From *Prehistoric Architecture in the Eastern United States* by William N. Morgan (Cambridge: The MIT Press, 1980).

the similarities between this piece and others found in the Mississippi Valley and Caddoan regions have given rise to speculation that all of these pieces may have been crafted in the same workshop, or at least in the same general area and by the same "school" of carvers, and later transported to other sites. According to Thomas Emerson of the University of Illinois Department of Anthropology, all of these pieces may originally have been carved as figurines, not as pipes. Neither the Birger nor the Keller figurine was made as a pipe, and the big boy–effigy pipe found at Spiro was not originally intended as a pipe but was modified by boring a hole through an already existing complicated relief pattern on the figure's cloak. According to Emerson, the major source of bauxite in the United States is in Arkansas, and he believes that the Birger and Keller pieces, the big boy, the chunkey player, and possibly the Shiloh pipe were carved somewhere in the Arkansas region and distributed through trade to the other sites as finished products (Emerson 1982, 8).

Certainly, the carvings have stylistic similarities that would seem to support this hypothesis. The artist's technique is in all cases assured and sophisti-

36. Mound at the Shiloh site, McNairy County, Tennessee. Photo by Barbara Gibbs.

cated and shows an understanding of naturalistic form. Various figurative elements, such as the facial features, the costume details, and the hair, have been simplified without sacrificing the representational accuracy of the work. Each piece has a feeling of animation, of incipient motion, and the position of the figures, kneeling and bending slightly forward, is the same. The pieces are all about the same size and date from around A.D. 1150. If not produced by the same artist or the same workshop, these works certainly represent a definite style in Mississippian figurative sculpture.

During the latter part of the Mississippian period, beginning around A.D. 1150, climate shifts resulted in warmer, wetter winters and cool, dry summers—conditions unfavorable to the cultivation of corn and other staple crops. Several scholars, among them David Brose, believe that these conditions had an increasingly negative impact on the stability of Mississippian society, especially in the heartland regions. "Relatively autonomous but weak social elites were forced to deal with internal disruptions, economic imbalances, and finally, alien occupation. Their role in structuring world-renewing

37. Lichens along the
trail, Shiloh site, McNairy
County, Tennessee.
Photo by Barbara Gibbs.

rituals was ever more critical, yet their role in the control and redistribution of economic information and products was lessening" (Galloway 1989, 30). According to Brose, much of the art produced during this period was one result of efforts to retain traditional cultural values in the face of changing economic and demographic conditions. By circa 1300 there was a trend toward conventionalization of subjects and styles, with fewer innovations and less experimentation. The renaissance was over, and a period of Mannerist elaboration had begun.

During the next phase (A.D. 1300–1500), there was an intensification of the warrior cult, especially in the Caddoan area. It was also during this period that the Southeastern Ceremonial Complex began to spread throughout the Southeast. There is a tendency toward increased regional variation as the long-distance trade system began to deteriorate. There are also fewer depictions of human forms and more emphasis on abstract symbols, perhaps associated with religious icons.

During the Late Mississippian phase (A.D. 1500–1700), there was a further reduction in diversity of subjects in art and a concentration on a few specific motifs, such as the rattlesnake, the piasa, the thunderbird, and the death mask. The Citico style of the Coosa, represented by conventionalized and abstracted rattlesnake designs, is characteristic of this phase (see figure 58). So is the Spaghetti style found along the Gulf Coast (see plate 22). Forms and patterns had become set. Repetition replaced innovation. Technical skill was still evident, but the creative spark had largely been extinguished. The artist had nothing new to say.

According to Lewis H. Larson, the Citico style represents the final vestige of the engraved shell tradition. "It appears that the shell gorget went out of style or was no longer manufactured after 1600" (Galloway 1989, 145). This was probably the result of a breakdown of organized craft specialization that had been supported by the Mississippian elite. Chiefly power had been severely eroded by this time, and there was a shift throughout the region to less-organized social structures. European intrusion and the spread of Old World diseases exacerbated this process, ultimately leading to the complete collapse of Mississippian society.

CHAPTER 5

Sacrifice and Ceremonialism
in the Lower Mississippi Valley

D riving south from Memphis along Mississippi's Route 1, the Great River Road, one passes through a seemingly endless expanse of flat green fields intersected by groves of deeper green trees. The serenity of the landscape has an almost hypnotic effect not unlike that of driving through the Great Western Desert, and at times Route 1 follows a line almost as straight as those grey ribbons of asphalt that inch across the wastelands of west Texas or the sandy, sage-littered tracts of eastern Nevada. By way of contrast, however, the Great Mississippi Valley is a desert of plenty, a great basin of fertility, one huge farm of row crops that stretch as far as the eye can see.

The potential fertility of the area, with its excellent sandy loam soil and long growing season, was not lost on the pre-Columbian inhabitants of the region. Their settlements grew up along the major waterways not only because of the possibilities for riverine trade and transportation but also because, as farmers, they knew good cropland when they saw it. Important Mississippian period settlements are liberally sprinkled along the length of the Great River and its tributaries from Aztalan in southern Wisconsin to Emerald in southern Mississippi. The remains of one of the largest and most impressive of these towns is located 150 miles south of Memphis near Greenville, Mississippi. We call it Winterville.

Originally, Winterville boasted at least twenty-three pyramidal mounds, of which twelve have been preserved (see figure 38). The largest—the Great Temple Mound—rises fifty-five feet above the surrounding plain. The town enjoyed a conveniently direct access to the Mississippi River by way of Deer Creek.

Unlike the Euro-Americans, who often built their towns on the banks of the Great River, then lived to regret it, the Native Americans had enormous respect for the mighty Mississippi and rarely, if ever, established themselves directly on its active channels. Winterville was also located on the highest elevation in the vicinity, making it relatively immune to all but the most disastrous of floods. The high land was also better drained and therefore agriculturally superior.

The Winterville Mounds are arranged in a rough oval around an enormous plaza, with the primary one, Mound A, located in the center of the oval (see figures 39 and 40). This unusual arrangement creates not one but two ceremonial plazas—one to the northeast of the central mound and the other to the southwest. Like Spiro, but unlike many other Mississippian towns, the mound area at Winterville is devoid of midden garbage and other debris, and therefore probably functioned primarily as a ceremonial center with only a small residential population of political and religious figures.

Part of the explanation for the unusual layout of the Winterville site may lie in the fact that the entire lower Yazoo Basin represented a markedly different type of Mississippian culture, a variation that has been labeled Plaquemine. Jeffrey Brain, in *Winterville: Late Prehistoric Culture Contact in the Lower Mississippi Valley*, provides an excellent assessment of the process that resulted in the "Mississippianization" of the region. Brain points out that the Winterville area was the meeting ground of two major cultural traditions—Coles Creek, which represented cultural patterns indigenous to the region, and the Mississippian tradition, which appears to have entered the Lower Mississippi Valley sometime in the eleventh century A.D.

The Coles Creek culture began to take shape around A.D. 500. The Coles Creek people were also moundbuilders but on a much more modest scale than

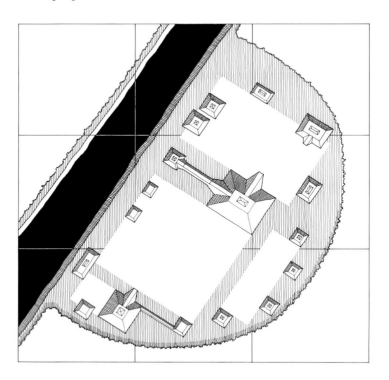

38. Winterville site, Greenville, Mississippi; Mississippian period, A.D. 1200–1350. From *Prehistoric Architecture in the Eastern United States* by William N. Morgan (Cambridge: The MIT Press, 1980).

their Mississippian counterparts. Brain writes, "By A.D. 1000, Coles Creek had expanded as far north as the latitude of the Arkansas River. At that time it appears to have been a strong, well-organized, remarkably homogeneous culture . . . which probably represented a well developed socio-political structure of closely interacting petty chiefdoms. The general lack of evidence . . . for influence from outside the area suggests that the people themselves were quite provincial in outlook and content with making a finely attuned, locally oriented adaptation to the rich alluvial bottomlands of the Lower Mississippi Valley" (Brain 1989, 4).

The mounds that the Coles Creek people built were small multipurpose affairs used as bases for structures as well as repositories for the dead. A typical site had an average of three modest mounds, which functioned primarily as a ceremonial center, with the general population dispersed in small villages throughout the area. The Coles Creek people were basically subsistence farmers who also engaged in hunting and fishing. They made clay-tempered pottery, lived in simple wood and mud huts, and followed a way of life that became entrenched for five hundred years.

40. Winterville site from
the top of the mound.
Photo by Barbara Gibbs.

Then, somewhere around A.D. 1000, change arrived. At several sites on the northern frontier of the Coles Creek culture, certain distinctive traits foreign to the area began to appear. These included special types of pottery that used shell instead of clay as a tempering agent, new vessel forms with looped handles and animal effigy heads, and possibly a new type of house construction. Shortly after the appearance of these innovations, a new group of people began moving into the area. They were Mississippians from the north, and they were to have an enormous impact on developments in the Lower River Valley for the next five hundred years.

It is not known for sure what prompted the movement of Mississippians into the Yazoo Basin, but scholars have speculated that demographic pressure—that is, overpopulation—in the Mississippian heartland may have encouraged migration. The new settlers generally moved into sparsely occupied areas and went about setting up their own villages, planting their fields, and practicing their Mississippian life-style. Comparable migrations seemed to be occurring elsewhere around the same time in northeast Arkansas and in the Macon Plateau region.

In many areas, contact with people of the Mississippian metropolis of

Cahokia is evident. Writes Brain, "In the Yazoo region there is firm evidence of direct contact from this center. . . . It is believed that motivations for the intrusion were primarily economic, although there may also have been a strong religious element" (Brain 1989, 129). The Cahokians, in other words, were the missionaries of the Mississippian way of life. Small core groups appear to have moved out from the area of southern Illinois into a broad region that included the Arkansas and Red River valleys to the west, the Tennessee River Valley to the east, the southern Appalachians, and the Mississippi River Valley, both north and south. This intrusion took many different forms, from what appears to have been a full-scale conquest in some areas to the peaceful infiltration that seems to have characterized the Mississippian presence in the Yazoo Basin. "The particular form . . . of the intrusion into the Yazoo region may have been dictated by the highly developed culture that was found there," writes Brain. "An arrogant imposition such as a site-unit intrusion may have been too difficult an undertaking in the face of organized resistance, while a more subtle approach . . . may have been deemed more effective" (Brain 1989, 129). Whatever the approach, the process was extremely effective. Within a short time, the entire Yazoo region was thoroughly "Mississippianized."

Because of its location, Winterville was a major conduit for the spread of Mississippian influence in the area via the Mississippi River, which helped distribute ideas as well as trade goods. Winterville, which began as a minor outpost on the frontier of the Coles Creek culture, was soon transformed into a major Mississippian town, one of the largest in the Southeast. The Coles Creek culture, successful as it had been in terms of subsistence farming and basic technology, was introverted and provincial compared with Mississippian society. What happened at Winterville and elsewhere in the region as a result of Mississippian infiltration represented a "grand local florescence," a great explosion of innovation and technological and ideological development.

Moreover, the Mississippian and Coles Creek cultures appear to have met peacefully, for there is no evidence of violence, no large-scale fortifications, no replacements of one culture by another. Instead, the Coles Creek people appeared to be receptive to Mississippian ideas, and the hybridization of the two cultures quickly developed into a highly successful tradition, which retained some elements of Coles Creek while incorporating the best that the Mississippians had to offer. "After the centuries of relative isolation, the Coles Creek peoples may have reacted to the Cahokia-Mississippian contact with an enthusiasm that was revolutionary" (Brain 1989, 132).

Even though the Winterville mounds are the remains of one of the largest Mississippian period towns in the Lower Mississippi River Valley, Winterville was surprisingly lacking in ceremonial artifacts. When archaeologist Clarence Moore came to Winterville in November 1907, he was hoping to discover a wealth of archaeologically significant artifacts comparable to those he had recently recovered from the Moundville site in Alabama. Accompanied by five highly trained laborers, he set to work digging more than 150 trial holes into the mounds and the flat areas between them. He was thoroughly disappointed with the results: only a few badly preserved skeletons and some relatively lackluster pots. His report of the excavation contains not a single illustration of an artifact, so meager were the findings.

Moore's loss was, however, science's gain, since the disappointing results of his initial excavation kept the site safe from pot hunters and treasure seekers for many years. Sporadic investigations were undertaken over the years, however, and enough interest was generated in the site to prompt the Greenville Garden Club to undertake a fund-raising venture aimed at securing the property for the public domain. In 1939 the City of Greenville purchased forty-two acres, representing about 80 percent of the site, and turned it into a park. In 1960, the park was taken over by the Mississippi State Park Commission, which has operated it ever since. The park now includes a museum, a picnic area, and interpretative displays to acquaint the visitor with the major features of the site.

The Winterville Mounds Museum contains a number of artifacts from the Clark collection that were excavated from sites in the Winterville area. One of the pieces, a stone effigy pipe, represents a bound captive. Although damaged, the figure is still remarkably graceful and likely comes from the same phase of Mississippian figurative sculpture seen at Cahokia, Spiro, and elsewhere in the heartland region. The nude figure's arms are drawn back and bound with ropes while the head is tilted up, thus putting the body into a position of enormous tension, which the artist has reinforced with the figure's grasping hands and rigid muscles. The overall impression once again is that of catching the figure in that critical moment just before the action takes place—perhaps, in this case, the moment just before the executioner's ax descends.

A second intriguing artifact from Winterville is an early representation (circa A.D. 1100) of a peregrine falcon, now at the Gilcrease Institute in Tulsa, Oklahoma. In this limestone pipe the falcon, symbol of the warrior elite, holds a severed head in its talons (see figure 41). The distinctive forked-eye marking is clearly evident, and the wings and beaded head are carved in deep relief. It would appear to be an early manifestation of the falcon-impersonator, which later found almost universal representation throughout the Mississippian world. Its presence at Winterville is one bit of evidence for the entrenchment there of the Mississippian "religion" and its cosmology of winged deities—birds, snakes, and panthers—which captured the imagination, and perhaps the devotion, of a quarter of the continent after the year A.D. 1000.

A hundred miles farther downriver are the remains of another unique town that provide further evidence of the innovative character of the Plaque-mine variant of Mississippian culture—a town called Emerald.

One of a number of Mississippian-style towns in the area, Emerald was apparently still occupied when the first European explorers arrived in the early 1500s. It is estimated that the mound complex was built between A.D. 1300 and 1600, rather late by Mississippian standards, and the plan differs from those of other sites. Located about ten miles north of present-day Natchez, Mississippi, the site covers almost eight acres and is the third largest mound in the United States. It is actually a series of mounds (eleven originally, of which only two are still readily visible) atop one megamound (see figures 42–44). The site was first explored by Cyrus Thomas for the Bureau of American Ethnology in 1884 and again in 1887. Thomas's report, published in 1894, mentions four mounds, but today the visitor will find only two—a large one, probably the temple mound, at the west end of the raised platform that forms a sort of artificial mesa, and a smaller mound at the east end (see figure 42). Excavations have indicated that additional smaller mounds, which probably served as the bases for impor-

41. Winterville falcon with severed human head, Washington County, Mississippi; Mississippian period, A.D. 1100–1200. From the Collection of Gilcrease Museum, Tulsa. Photo by Zena Pearlstone.

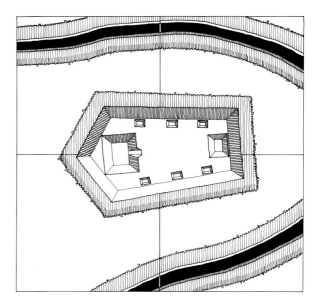

42. Emerald site, Stanton, Mississippi; Late Mississippian period, A.D. 1400–1700. From *Prehistoric Architecture in the Eastern United States* by William N. Morgan (Cambridge: The MIT Press, 1980).

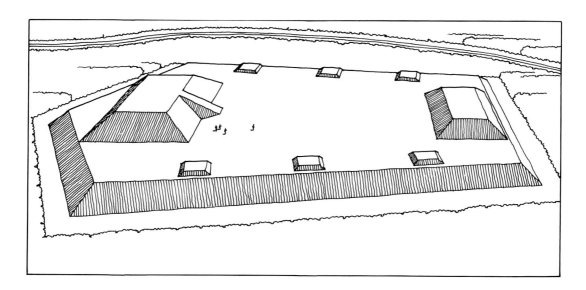

tant public buildings and residences of the elite, were placed along the edges of the plaza. In this unconventional arrangement, the entire ceremonial-political complex was elevated above the surrounding area, reinforcing the importance of the sacred institutions and those associated with their maintenance. The artificial mesa may also have made the ceremonial area easier to defend.

Two stone pipes associated with the Emerald site portray kneeling figures

43. Emerald site, Stanton, Mississippi. Photo by Barbara Gibbs.

44. The mound atop the mound, Emerald site. Photo by Barbara Gibbs.

similar to that of the pipe from Winterville. A limestone pipe which dates from around A.D. 1300, now in the Milwaukee Public Museum, represents a crouching man with his arms clasped across his chest. A second pipe in the form of a crouching man trussed up with ropes may represent a prisoner of war destined for execution (see figure 45). In both cases the figures are carved rather simply and retain the box-like shape of the stone blank. Neither is as elegant as the

Winterville prisoner, but all three appear to illustrate the same concept—the sacrifice or execution of a captive. It is interesting to compare these figures with the illustration of a Timucuan execution by the French artist-explorer Jacques Le Moyne that portrays a kneeling prisoner awaiting his fate (see figure 46). Le Moyne describes the event as follows: "The chief takes his place alone on his bench, those next to him in authority being seated on another long bench curved in a half circle; and the executioner orders the culprit to kneel down before the chief. He then sets his left foot on the delinquent's back, and, taking in both hands a club of ebony or some other hard wood, worked to an edge at the sides, he strikes him on the head with it, so severely as almost to split the skull open" (Swanton 1922, 380).

The description of the execution of a Natchez war prisoner noted by Antoine la Page du Pratz is also of interest. "If male prisoners are taken, the Natchez warriors go at once to hunt for the three poles which are necessary for the construction of the fatal instrument on which they are going to make the enemy they have taken die." Du Pratz goes on to say that after the prisoner's final meal, the warrior who actually captured him "gives a blow of his wooden war club below the back part of his head, making the death cry. Having thus stunned him he cuts the skin around his hair, puts his knees on his forehead, takes his hair in both hands, pulls it from the skull, and makes the death cry while removing the scalp in the best manner he is able without tearing it" (Crutchfield 1985, 51).

Both Emerald and the Grand Village of the Natchez were located along the Natchez Trace, a 450-mile-long trail that linked three of the largest watercourses in the United States—the Cumberland, Tennessee, and Mississippi rivers. Beginning just south of the Cumberland near present-day Nashville, the trail led southwest across the Tennessee River Valley, the northern Alabama highlands, and on to the low bluffs along the eastern bank of the Mississippi near present-day Natchez (see figures 47 and 48 and map 2).

The trail spans a wide diversity of ecological zones, ranging from the mixed deciduous forests and mountainous terrain of the highlands to the low-lying swamps and marshes of the Deep South. According to James Crutchfield, author of *The Natchez Trace: A Pictorial History,* at least 100 species of trees, 215 species of birdlife, 57 species of mammals, and 89 species of reptiles and amphibians reside along the trail. During Mississippian times, the trace undoubtedly served as a main north-south artery in the vast trade network that connected the ceremonial centers and their satellite villages. At the southern terminus of the trail was the Grand Village of the Natchez.

Located on the banks of St. Catherine Creek, the Grand Village of the Natchez has been partially restored and is currently maintained by the Mississippi Department of Archives and History (see figure 49). Most of our knowl-

45. Bound captive, human-effigy pipe, sandstone, Emerald site, Stanton, Mississippi; Mississippian period, A.D. 1300–1500. Acc. no. 37.2802. Courtesy of The Brooklyn Museum, New York; the Henry L. Batterman Fund and the Frank Sherman Benson Fund.

46. Execution of a prisoner; after Le Moyne. Courtesy of Rare Books and Manuscripts Division, The New York Public Library/Astor, Lenox, and Tilden Foundations.

47. The Natchez Trace, near Natchez, Mississippi. Photo by Barbara Gibbs.

edge about the old capital of the Natchez tribe comes from the written accounts of early European visitors.

In 1703, the Frenchman Jean Penicaut wrote in his journal, "We paid a visit to the Natchez, one of the most polite and affable nations on the Mississippi. They inhabit one of the most beautiful countries in Louisiana [as it was then called] which lies about a league from the banks of the Mississippi, and is embellished with magnificent natural scenery, covered with a splendid growth of odoriferous trees and plants, and watered with cool and limpid streams. This nation is composed of thirty villages, but the one we visited was the largest, because it contained the dwelling of the Great Chief, whom they call the Sun, which means noble" (Penicaut, in Swanton 1911).

Another early settler, Antoine la Page du Pratz (who had some training as an architect), paid close attention to the architectural setting of the inhabitants' complex social and ceremonial life. "The cabins of the natives," he wrote, "are all perfectly square. There is not one that measures less than 15 feet each

48. Along the Natchez
Trace. Photo by Barbara
Gibbs.

way, but there are some more than 30. . . . The natives go into the young
woods in search of poles of young walnut [hickory] trees 4 inches in diameter
by 18 to 20 feet long. They plant the largest at the four corners to fix the
dimensions and the size of the dome" (Nabokov and Easton 1989, 96). After
the wall frame was constructed, the workers bent the extended corner poles
together to form a high, bowed roof frame "giving the whole the appearance
of a bower in a greenhouse." Canes were lashed to the frame, and over them
was plastered clay mixed with Spanish moss to create thick, durable walls.
Cane mats were fitted over the outside, and the roof was thatched with grass
"clipped uniformly, and in this way, however high the wind may be, it can do
nothing against the cabin. These coverings last twenty years without repair-
ing" (Nabokov and Easton 1989, 96).

The Natchez preoccupation with social hierarchy was apparent in their
architecture, as was the case at most other Mississippian sites. At the Grand
Village, temples and the residences of the elite were typically built on mounds

49. Fatherland site,
Grand Village of the
Natchez near Natchez,
Mississippi. Photo by
Barbara Gibbs.

surrounding the plaza. However, as with other sites in the Lower Mississippi Valley, the ground plan of the Grand Village is atypical in that there are two plazas. While the layout of the buildings is reminiscent of Winterville, it would appear from the evidence that the double plaza was the result not of planning but of unforeseen circumstances: the original temple mound, located at the north end of the plaza, was abandoned for some unknown reason, and a new temple mound was constructed to the south. The residence of the Great Sun, which had originally stood at the south end of the plaza, was moved to the north end of the new plaza. All three structures were bounded on the east by St. Catherine Creek, a tributary of the Mississippi. Du Pratz noted that a temple guardian lived permanently in the ceremonial precinct, tending a perpetual fire of logs, which was "revered as a fragment of the divine sun itself." Du Pratz's friend, Tattooed Serpent, the Great War Chief and brother of the Great Sun, lived in a centrally located house that commanded a full view of the surroundings. "He occupied a building 30 feet long and 20 feet high from the tamped earth floor to thatched roof. Its wattle and daub construction was without windows, but beautifully woven mats covered the interior walls" (Nabokov and Easton 1989, 97). "The Natchez," observed du Pratz, "are brought up in a most perfect submission to their sovereign; the authority which their princes exercise over them is absolutely despotic" (Stuart 1988, 49).

1. Panther-effigy pipe, steatite, Copena culture; Middle Woodland period, A.D. 1–400. Photo by Dirk Baaker, The Detroit Institute of Arts. Acc. no. L49.5. Anonymous loan to The Brooklyn Museum, New York.

2. Crystal River mound, Citrus County, Florida. Photo by Barbara Gibbs.

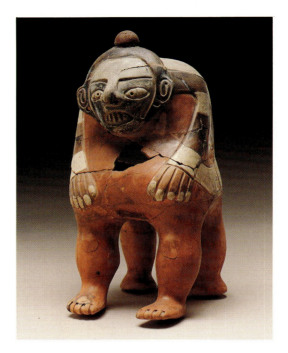

3. Human-effigy urn, polychrome ceramic, Buck Mound, Fort Walton Beach, Florida; Weeden Island period, A.D. 500–800. Photo by Dirk Baaker, The Detroit Institute of Arts. Courtesy of the Indian Temple Mound Museum, Fort Walton Beach, Florida.

4. Burial mound, Kolomoki mounds, Early County, Georgia. Photo by Barbara Gibbs.

5. Monks Mound, Cahokia mounds near Collinsville, Illinois. Photo by Barbara Gibbs.

6. Charnel house platform and burial mound, Cahokia. Photo by Barbara Gibbs.

7. Stockade at Cahokia. Photo by Barbara Gibbs.

8. Birger figurine, bauxite, BBB Motor site, Madison County, Illinois; Mississippian culture, Sterling phase, Cahokia area, A.D. 1000–1250. Photo by Dirk Baaker, The Detroit Institute of Arts. Courtesy of the Illinois Department of Transportation, Springfield.

10. Big boy–effigy pipe, bauxite, Spiro phase, Caddoan culture; Mississippian period, A.D. 1200–1350. Photo by Dirk Baaker, The Detroit Institute of Arts. Courtesy of the University Museum, University of Arkansas, Fayetteville.

9. Repoussé plaque with dancing figures, copper, Bluff Lake Area, Union County, Illinois; Mississippian period, A.D. 1100–1300. Photo by Dirk Baaker, The Detroit Institute of Arts. Courtesy of the Department of Anthropology, Smithsonian Institution, Washington, D.C., catalogue no. 88142.

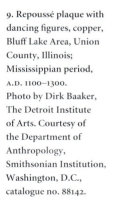

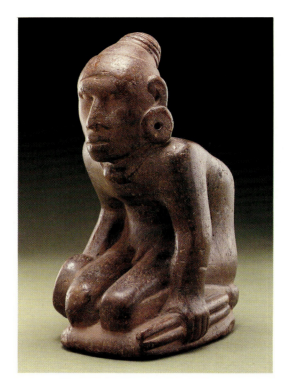

11. Chunkey player–effigy pipe, bauxite, Caddoan culture; Mississippian period, A.D. 1200–1350. Photo by Dirk Baaker, The Detroit Institute of Arts. From the collections of the St. Louis Science Center, St. Louis, Missouri.

12. Mounds at Shiloh. Photo by Barbara Gibbs.

13. The Tennessee River as seen from the Shiloh mounds near Shiloh, Tennessee. Photo by Barbara Gibbs.

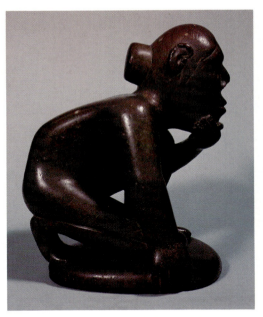

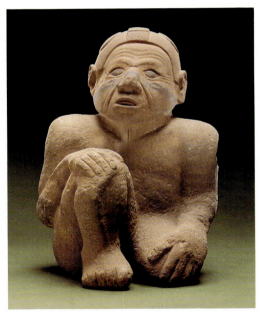

14. Human-effigy pipe, bauxite, Shiloh site, McNairy County, Tennessee; Mississippian period, A.D. 1000–1250. Courtesy of the National Park Service, Shiloh National Military Park, Tennessee.

15. Seated male figure, sandstone, Wilson County, Tennessee; Late Mississippian period, A.D. 1300–1500. Photo by Dirk Baaker, The Detroit Institute of Arts. Courtesy of the Frank H. McClung Museum, University of Tennessee, Knoxville.

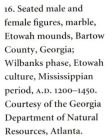

16. Seated male and female figures, marble, Etowah mounds, Bartow County, Georgia; Wilbanks phase, Etowah culture, Mississippian period, A.D. 1200–1450. Courtesy of the Georgia Department of Natural Resources, Atlanta.

17. The Temple Mound at Etowah near Cartersville, Georgia. Photo by Barbara Gibbs.

18. Mounds reflected in the Etowah River, Etowah site near Cartersville, Georgia. Photo by Barbara Gibbs.

19. Mound at Etowah. Photo by Barbara Gibbs.

20. Mounds at Ocmulgee, Macon, Georgia. Photo by Barbara Gibbs.

21. Mounds at Ocmulgee. Photo by Barbara Gibbs.

22. Spaghetti-style
engraved shell gorget,
marine shell, Dallas site,
Hamilton County,
Tennessee; Dallas
culture, Late Mississip-
pian period, A.D. 1300–
1500. Photo by Dirk
Baaker, The Detroit
Institute of Arts.
Courtesy of the Frank H.
McClung Museum,
University of Tennessee,
Knoxville.

23. The plaza at Town Creek, Montgomery County, North Carolina. Photo by Barbara Gibbs.

24. Reconstruction of the plaza and temple mound at the Town Creek site, Montgomery County, North Carolina. Photo by Barbara Gibbs.

25. Inside the stockade at Town Creek. Photo by Barbara Gibbs.

26. Reconstruction at the Town Creek site, Montgomery County, North Carolina. Photo by Barbara Gibbs.

27. Interior of the reconstructed "Chief's House" showing wattle and daub construction, Town Creek site, Montgomery County, North Carolina. Photo by Barbara Gibbs.

28. Mound at the Fort Watson site near Santee, North Carolina. Photo by Barbara Gibbs.

29. Marine shell bowl (Pensacola Incised), ceramic, Choctawhatchee Bay, Walton County, Florida; Fort Walton culture, Late Mississippian period, A.D. 1350–1500. Photo by Dirk Baaker, The Detroit Institute of Arts. Courtesy of the Temple Mound Museum, Fort Walton Beach, Florida.

30. Fort Walton/Safety Harbor bowl, ceramic, Walton County, Florida; Fort Walton culture, Late Mississippian period, A.D. 1350–1500. Temple Mound Museum, Fort Walton Beach, Florida. Photo by Barbara Gibbs.

31. View of Tampa Bay
from the Safety Harbor
site. Photo by Barbara
Gibbs.

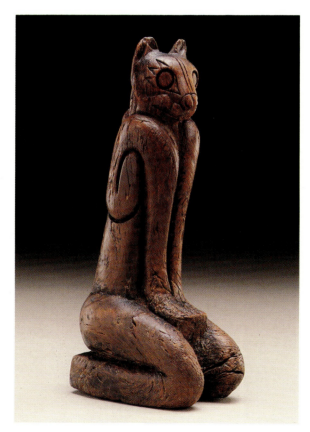

32. Kneeling feline,
wood, Key Marco site,
Collier County, Florida;
Calusa culture, A.D.
1000–1400. Photo by
Dirk Baaker, The Detroit
Institute of Arts.
Courtesy of the Depart-
ment of Anthropology,
Smithsonian Institution,
Washington, D.C.
Catalogue no. 88142.

It seems clear from these accounts that, at least among the Natchez and the Timucuans, the Mississippian people were ruled by divinely sanctioned aristocrats who administered the state, the military, and religion. This supposition is reinforced by archaeological evidence from a number of sites throughout the Southeast including Cahokia, where the "life and death power of one class over another is clearly demonstrated . . . by the mass graves filled with the retainers in Mound 72" (Fowler 1974, 98).

According to du Pratz, the Great Sun of the Natchez claimed divine descent from the sun itself. He wore a crown of white feathers, and his subjects carried him about in a flower-covered litter. When he dined, the most revered members of the hierarchy sat at his feet, and when he was finished eating, he used his feet to move the bowls in their direction so they could partake of the chiefly repast. "Our nation," the Great Sun told du Pratz, "was formerly very numerous and very powerful. It extended more than twelve days journey from east to west, and more than fifteen from south to north" (Stuart 1988, 49).

The Grand Village of the Natchez was one of the last remaining Mississippian towns still in existence at the time of European contact. The rest had been abandoned, the old ways had been lost, and the history and traditions had dissolved into vague memories and disjointed myths. But at the Grand Village, some of the old ways may have been preserved despite the ravages of disease and increasing conflict with the invading Europeans.

It is important, however, to keep in mind that the Natchez were but one small group of Mississippianized people living on the fringes of what had been an enormous zone of Mississippian cultural influence. Also, most Mississippian ceremonial centers had long since been abandoned by the time du Pratz and his contemporaries arrived among the Natchez. Despite the intriguing connections that might well exist between the postcontact remnants of Mississippian civilization and its earlier manifestations, it is dangerous to assume a direct link. In trying to capture the essence of Mississippian civilization, we have been forced to rely heavily on the reports of European adventurers whose perceptions and interpretations may have been distorted by their own ethnocentric views. They saw what was left of Mississippian culture through the lens of European preoccupation with class and conquest—a view which might or might not correspond to the realities of Mississippian life. They may be forgiven for trying to understand an exotic foreign culture by making analogies with political and religious systems with which they were familiar, but we must not fail to take into account their prejudices and preconceptions in our own quest to better interpret the evidence of archaeological facts.

NOT QUITE TWELVE foot-days' journey to the east of the Grand Village of the Natchez are the ruins of another grand Mississippian town that may also have been inhabited when de Soto passed close by in the summer of 1540. Without doubt one of the most beautiful and impressive of all of the Mississippian towns, it is known today as Moundville.

The first extensive accounts of Moundville date from the early nineteenth century, a time when many people still entertained the theory that the numerous mounds that dotted the countryside were the work of a vanished race that had preceded the Native Americans—the survivors of Atlantis, perhaps, or one of the Ten Lost Tribes of Israel. Educated people passing through northern Alabama noted the ruins of an ancient town and named the place Carthage after the North African city destroyed by the Romans in 146 B.C. The site was known as the Carthage Mounds until late in the nineteenth century.

The earliest excavations of the Moundville site were carried out by Clarence Moore, who traveled to the region in the winter of 1905 and was impressed by what he saw. He returned the next year and spent two months excavating extensively. He was rewarded with such a wealth of splendid artifacts that Moundville soon became one of the most famous archaeological sites in the Southeast. This, in turn, led to the systematic looting of the site by a host of treasure seekers until, by the early 1920s, the place seemed doomed to complete destruction.

Then in 1923, a group of local citizens began a campaign to protect the site, and in 1929 the Alabama Museum of Natural History Board of Regents began to buy up the land surrounding the mounds. The founder of the group, state geologist and museum director Walter Jones, even mortgaged his own home to raise money for the purchase. Subsequently, the land was donated to the State of Alabama, and in 1933 Mound State Park was established.

Today, Mound State Monument is under the protection of the University of Alabama, which has overseen a number of excavations in the area. These efforts have resulted in the recovery of literally thousands of artifacts as well as pottery fragments, the remains of seventy-five houses, and numerous other bits and pieces of archaeologically significant material.

At its height in the late thirteenth century, Moundville may have had a resident population of as many as 3,000 people. The town, built on a high bluff overlooking a curve of the Black Warrior River, included at least twenty mounds scattered over a 300-acre area (see figures 50–52). Surrounding a large rectangular plaza—the center of life at Moundville—were domestic dwellings, large public buildings, and two mortuary houses. The plaza itself contained ball courts, areas for public events, and markets where farm produce may have been traded for pottery and other items manufactured in the town. There was also a rectangular building thought to be a sweathouse. A palisade, its bastions arranged for advantageous crossfire, protected the city center.

The satellite villages that both supported Moundville and depended on it stretched along some seventy-five miles of river valley, adding perhaps 10,000 or more subjects to Moundville's jurisdiction. These dependencies made Moundville the largest settlement in the Southeast for its time, and one archaeologist has called it the "Big Apple of 14th century North America" (Stuart 1988, 37). On ceremonial occasions, people from the surrounding area would have gathered at Moundville, approaching it along well-worn paths. Imagine the thrill of emerging from the dense primordial forest and seeing before you the splendid city of mounds with its temples rising into the sky. Sculptures of fierce birds and feathered serpents guarded the sacred buildings, copper eyes glinting in the sun. Imagine the throngs of people on festival days. In the ceremonial plaza, costumed dancers performed, and the crowds cheered the players in the ball game. At night, thousands of campfires would have gleamed from the surrounding hills like clusters of stars. And at first light, the cries of the priests would have echoed from the tops of the mounds, announcing the rising sun that marked the great cycles of planting and harvest, of death and rebirth, of destruction and renewal.

50. Moundville site, Moundville, Alabama; Mississippian period, A.D. 1200–1500. From *Prehistoric Architecture in the Eastern United States* by William N. Morgan (Cambridge: The MIT Press, 1980).

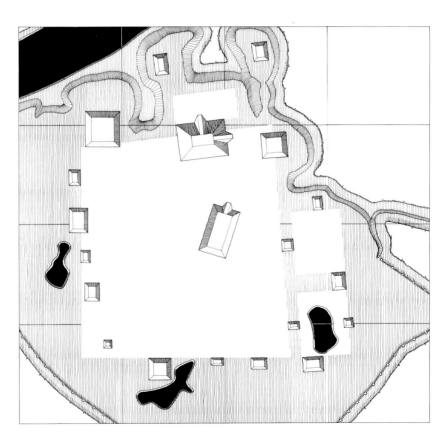

In summer, the people may have celebrated the first harvest with agricultural rituals, which might have formed the basis for the Green Corn Ceremony of early historic times. During the Green Corn Ceremony, old fires were extinguished and new ones lit at a sacred hearth in the temple, with part of the flames taken home to distant villages. Thus, all of the people were united, all shared in a network of rights and obligations, rituals and relationships. Joseph Vogel, director of the Alabama Museum of Natural History, writes:

> Rulers and ruled alike were caught up in a social fabric of mutual obligation reenforced by the dual threads of economic interdependence and kin allegiances. Chiefs at all levels had broad rights of request for food, goods and services, while being generally responsible for the group's welfare. Each chief, sub-chief, or village headman served as a local leader as well as a conduit for decisions made at higher levels. These decisions involved him in the recruitment of labor for socially beneficial projects, the organization of religious festivals, and the mediation of disputes between group members or defense against enemies. . . . The chief had a retinue of wives, retainers, and assistants, and contact with him was restricted by elaborate rules of protocol. The life of the chief—birth, marriage, and especially death—were usually accompanied by public rituals. (Walthall and Vogel 1982, 5)

Once again, Vogel's remarks are based on extrapolations of historic information gathered during the last phases of a dying culture. Art historian Amelia Trevelyan has pointed out that it is important to keep in mind what we know today about the dissolution of complex societies—that dying regimes often tend to become more strict and tyrannical in the attempt to maintain their control. The historical accounts on which we have based many of our suppositions about Mississippian culture may actually be *atypical* of earlier Mississippian society. The emphasis on social hierarchies and military activities and the despotic posture of leaders such as the Natchez's Great Sun may not provide accurate blueprints for reconstructing earlier Mississippian customs (Trevelyan, personal communication).

Moundville, along with Etowah and Spiro, yielded the largest and most elaborate cache of artifacts created by Mississippian artists. Thus it has played a major role in the formation of theories regarding Mississippian religion, specifically the Southeastern Ceremonial Complex. Certainly, Moundville art appears to have been inspired by religious ideology and was associated for the most part with the ruling elite of Moundville society. A distinctive "Moundville style" can be detected having certain key elements, such as the skull, long bones, rattlesnake, and other death motifs that appear again and again on pottery, stone palettes, and various other artifacts. The cross-and-circle, hand-

51. Moundville site, Moundville, Alabama. Photo by Barbara Gibbs.

eye, bi-lobed arrow, and bird-man were other favorite elements of Moundville artists.

Especially striking are a number of black-filmed ceramic pieces apparently manufactured at Moundville. A graceful shallow bowl, now in the University of Alabama Museum, is decorated with alternating hands and forearm bones incised along the rim. Another engraved ceramic piece, now in the Alabama Museum of Natural History, features a hand-eye motif. The design was scratched on the surface of the pot after it was fired, revealing the lighter-colored core. Using this method the artist could create intricate designs and a striking positive/negative effect.

Another celebrated example of the Moundville style of pottery is a beaker decorated with a skull and long bone motif (see figure 53). The skull is abstracted to an almost cartoon-like mask with bared teeth and what may be earrings. A design on the top of the head might represent a headdress, although it could also be a representation of scalping.

Stone palettes, several of them quite large, are another intriguing example of Moundville artistry. It is thought that these elegant disks were used for mixing paints for ritual use, and small jars of ground pigments were also discovered at the site. The stone disks are decorated with ceremonial symbols including the hand-eye, knotted rattlesnake, bi-lobed arrow, skull, and long bones. The designs were engraved into the dark stone and filled with light paste so that the palettes resemble the incised ceramics that bear the same motifs (see figure 54).

"It isn't easy climbing into the heads of these people," notes University of Alabama archaeologist V. J. Knight, "but we have learned so much in the past decade. For instance, a few art motifs are abstract and don't have any obvious factual reference. I think they're specific glyphs for water, for the underworld, among other things. I don't know if you want to call it writing, but certain symbols were like glyphs—standard ways of representing concepts, which is writing in a sense" (Stuart 1988, 45).

52. Vine-covered mounds at Moundville. Photo by Barbara Gibbs.

53. Beaker with skull and long bones, ceramic, Moundville site, Hale County, Alabama; Mississippian period, A.D. 1400–1500. Photo by Dirk Baaker, The Detroit Institute of Arts; courtesy of Alabama Museum of Natural History, Tuscaloosa.

Moundville, although still functioning in the early 1500s, followed the pattern of decline that was the fate of Mississippian cities throughout the Southeast—central authority diminished and the society dispersed into the fragmented groups encountered by European settlers. This process probably had many contributing factors, including an underlying lack of support from the general populace as well as increasing pressures from European intrusion. The spread of Old World diseases may also have contributed to the breakdown of Mississippian society.

At least one theory cites population growth as a factor in the decline of Mississippian society. Joseph Vogel writes:

The fragmentation of Mississippian society and the demise of Moundville coincided with a reduction of the authority of chiefly families resident there. This diminished their ability to construct monumental public works and engage in other elite activities. The loss of authority is related to the

54. Engraved stone
palette, Moundville site,
Hale County, Alabama;
Mississippian period,
A.D. 1200–1500. Photo
by Dirk Baaker, The
Detroit Institute of Arts;
courtesy of Alabama
Museum of Natural
History, Tuscaloosa.

significant population growth within the chiefdom. Population growth in
a society based on kinship means that through time proportionately fewer
people are born with close relationship to the chiefly line. Indeed, as
growth continues, most people can claim only faint kinship and can enjoy
little benefit from it. This increasing social distance of the majority of the
population from the paramount chief tends to do two things: it reduces
the benefits of close relationship—participation in elite activities, prestige, and influence, while undercutting the flow of goods and services. . . .
Thus, as the tokens of chiefly prestige diminished among the long standing elite families, new kin-allegiances arose as people recognized obligations to emerging chiefly lineages closer to home. (Walthall and Vogel
1982, 10)

Vogel also points out that the Mississippian hierarchy was supported by farming, and that since the religious and political structure required belief in the idea that a good harvest was due to the intercession of the chief, crops failures would also be attributed to him. Several years of drought would reduce crop production and undermine the belief in the validity of the religious system. As the system failed, authority fell into the hands of petty chieftains, and the regional organization of the society came to an end. "Without tribute flowing into Moundville, many notable activities ceased: construction and maintenance of the substructure mounds, fortifications, barrow pits, and harbors. Much of the ritual, authority and commerce moved to other centers, and the size of the resident population decreased. . . . Stripped of its reason for being, the town was reduced to a small settlement and slowly abandoned, [and soon] the Indian town of Moundville was no more" (Walthall and Vogel 1982, 11).

CHAPTER 6

The Cult
of the Ancestors

T HE INDIANS are a race of pagans and idolaters" wrote Garcilaso de la Vega. "They worship the sun and the moon as their principal deities. . . . They do have temples but they use them as sepulchres and not as houses of prayer. Moreover, because of the great size of these structures, they let them serve to hold the best and richest of their possessions. Their veneration for the temples and burial places, therefore, is most profound. On the doors of them they place the trophies of victories won over their enemies" (Varner and Varner 1980, 14).

The temple mound was the focal point of the Mississippian town. Its central location, its size, and the amount of physical labor required for its construction all point to its significance in the life of the Mississippian people. The cathedral town of medieval Europe is an appropriate analogy, for like the cathedral, the Mississippian temple mound dominated the landscape, a visible symbol of spiritual and political authority (see plate 24).

Just as the cathedral was a repository for holy relics—the remains of saints, the possessions of the honored dead, symbolic objects of historic significance in the life of the faithful—the temple mound was likewise the focal point for the veneration of the ancestors of the elite and the resting place for the holy relics that sustained the Mississippian social structure.

Most of us are interested in knowing something about our ancestors. A knowledge of our family history—where we came from, what our forebears accomplished, what they looked like—gives us a sense of identity, a context within which we can build our own personal history. In Mississippian times, the role of the ancestors—especially the ancestors of the ruling family—was magnified tremendously. The entire community found its identity through its attachment to the leader and his kin. Individual identity was unimportant compared to the common identity of the group. One's role in life, one's work, the selection of a mate—these were determined by one's place in the social hierarchy. While some flexibility may have existed in the order of obligations and relationships, the Mississippian social system was a tidy little universe with carefully delineated boundaries.

This order was reflected in the structure of the town itself. Like the concentric circles that form on the face of a pond when a pebble is dropped, the town grew outward from the center and the temple mound was at the heart. Everything else was connected to it and defined by its distance from this symbolic core. Around the temple mound were grouped the lesser mounds that housed the bones of the honored dead or served as foundations for the houses of public officials, priests, and military leaders. Tradesmen and artisans who served the elite were probably housed nearby. A palisade enclosed this inner circle, providing a visual and symbolic barrier between the rulers and the rest of the community (see plate 25). Beyond the palisade were the huts of the farmers, and beyond them the fields of corn and beans and squash in which the farmers labored. The farther from the center of power, the farther from the family of the Sun. And yet each ring of the circle was crucial to the whole. Devotion to the ruling family and veneration of the honored dead made up the glue that held the circle together. James Brown writes:

> From a political perspective, the most important formally constituted cult in southeastern societies was that organized around the veneration of the ancestors of the elite. It had as its cult headquarters a house or shrine where cult paraphernalia was stored when not in use. Such shrines . . . were the repositories of the elite dead, generally in the form of a selection of cleaned and dried bones. . . .
>
> Each of the items deposited in the shrine houses was one that could readily be used for political purposes. The fetishes and ancestral bones represented the ultimate sacred relics. The coppers, pearls, and other sumptuary objects were tools for economic development and the means for making foreign alliances. Armaments held the potential for coercive action. These shrines . . . were treated in the early historic period with notable respect and fear inspired by the powerful supernatural forces that resided with the illustrious dead. The cult leader, as senior descendant of these dead, naturally derived considerable power through his embodiment of sacred forces, and the priests who helped him tend the shrine . . . shared in the chief's elite status. (Brown 1985, 104)

Death is one of the most perplexing problems faced by our species, and the many and varied attempts to understand the process and its meaning have resulted in an endless assortment of belief systems and rituals. Since our earliest ancestors first sprinkled red ochre on the graves of their kin and left offerings of flowers and food for the deceased to use in the "afterlife," we have envisioned the possibility of something more beyond the closed door of the grave. We have built powerful religious systems on the basis of such theories and have created countless works of art to reinforce their credibility. Even today, using the tools of contemporary science, we continue to probe for the answer to the big question, an answer that eludes us despite our increased technological sophistication.

As we have seen, rituals of the dead played a central role in Mississippian society, as indeed they had during the preceding Woodland phase. Myths, legends, and complex ceremonial procedures affirmed the social relationships and duties between families, clans, and leaders. Burial offerings indicated the status of the deceased and attested to the families' position in the social structure of the group, while funerary rituals marked the rite of passage from life to death and ensured that the spirit of the deceased would move peacefully from one state to the next.

During the Woodland period in North America, a basic pattern of beliefs and rituals was established that was later modified to conform to new conditions during the Mississippian phase of development. Art historian David Penney writes:

> Since mortuary ritual helped define the identity of the social group, be it family, clan, or band, it was important to schedule the ceremony so that the entire group could participate. . . . Bodies had to be preserved and cared for until such time as it became appropriate to perform the funeral ceremony. Their preservation prior to a final mortuary ritual became an important element in the ceremonial preparation of the dead, and a pattern of re-burial or "bundle burial" became common during the Late Archaic period. As the dead accumulated between funerals, the ranks of mourners expanded, making the final ceremony relevant to more members of the group. If a funeral became more extravagant, more time might be necessary to gather together the resources for a significant ceremony. Meanwhile the dead had to be cared for until the ritual could be performed. One solution to this problem was the mortuary crypt or charnel house. (Penney 1985, 167)

Penney goes on to point out that the preparation of the body for burial and the housing of the prepared remains required a considerable amount of time and attention, probably resulting in the formation of a specialized group whose role in the society was to care for the honored dead. Several examples of Hopewell art illustrate the importance of mortuary practices, including references to deliberate disarticulation of the body prior to burial. Copper and mica cutouts depict headless, limbless torsos, and a unique stone sculpture from the Newark site in Ohio depicts a figure "dressed in a bear costume with a detached head on his lap" (see figure 55). "Here is an illustration of an

55. Wray figurine, stone, Licking County, Ohio; Middle Woodland period, 200 B.C.–A.D. 500. Ohio Historical Society, Columbus.

episode of mortuary ritual in which a religious practitioner performs rites over the disarticulated remains of the deceased" (Penney 1985, 170).

Many of these practices were continued during the Mississippian period. While most Mississippian individuals were buried in community cemeteries or beneath the floors of their homes, the remains of members of the high-status families were placed in special mortuary temples, similar to the Woodland charnel houses, when they died. Hernando de Soto and other early visitors to the Southeast described temples on top of large platform mounds that contained the remains of the ancestors of the chief, kept in baskets and cared for by priests. Stone, terra cotta, or wooden images, possibly depicting the deceased or the founding ancestor or "culture hero" of the chiefly lineage, guarded the receptacles of bones. After a long interval the accumulated remains of the dead were buried in the floor of the temple or around the circumference of the platform mound. Then the temple was destroyed, the entire mound covered with a fresh mantle of earth, and a new temple erected on top. During this episode of renewal, temple idols often received burial treatment much like the honored dead.

Representations of founding ancestors have been recovered from sites throughout the Southeast, with especially intriguing examples coming from Spiro, Etowah, and the Tennessee-Cumberland region. The ancestor is usually represented by a kneeling or seated figure, often with the hands resting on the knees. Whereas in the Caddoan sites the figures are exclusively males, sites in Illinois, Kentucky, Tennessee, and Georgia have often yielded pairs of figures— one male and one female.

Garcilaso de la Vega's account of the de Soto expedition mentions that male and female figures were commonly found in mortuary temples. He states that above each burial within the temple "was a statue carved from wood and placed on a pedestal against the wall. This was a personal likeness of the man or woman . . . and was made at the age he or she had attained at death" (Varner and Varner 1980).

Stylistically, these tomb sculptures adhere to roughly the same boundaries established by engraved and embossed objects. A seated male figure carved in wood found at the Spiro site is a good example of the Caddoan style (see figure 34). In contrast to the bauxite pipes from the same area, such as the chunkey player and big boy, the wood figure seems frozen and lifeless. The mouth is half open, the eyes stare straight ahead, and the body is stiff and rigid. The lack of fluidity is clearly not due to any lack of skill on the part of the artist but rather represents a meaningful appreciation of the differences between a living being and a dead one.

This same understanding is demonstrated in a kneeling male figure from Wilson County, Tennessee, now in the Frank McClung Museum at the University of Tennessee, Knoxville (see plate 15). Carved from sandstone and measuring nearly twenty inches high, the figure is shown with the right knee raised, a posture characteristic of mortuary statues from the Tennessee-Cumberland region. Although the man's face is very distinctive—rather portly with plump cheeks, a broad nose, and carefully delineated wrinkles—the mouth is in the same half-open position as that of the Spiro statue, and the eyes are vacant and staring. Traces of pigment on both statues indicate that they were originally painted.

Without doubt, the most spectacular examples of mortuary sculpture were found at the Etowah site in north-central Georgia. Here, in the base of what archaeologists called Mound C, two massive stone figures—a man and a woman—had been laid to rest along with the remains of more than 200 others, as well as thousands of artifacts made from copper, shell, ceramic, and wood (see plate 16). It is thought that Mound C formed the base for the mortuary temple and that the burials represented the accumulated remains of generations of Mississippian leaders and their families. The two statues, carved from Georgia marble, may well have been the funerary portraits of the founding ancestors, the Mother and Father of the people of Etowah.

Whoever they represent, they are an impressive couple. Nearly three feet high, the kneeling figures are close to life-size. The man's legs are crossed, while the woman's legs are tucked under her. She wears a short skirt with a belted waist and a neatly folded headdress that hangs like a veil down her back. The man's headdress is a cap-like affair with folds or pleats on the sides of the crown. There is evidence that both figures were originally painted and probably decorated with copper ornaments and other costume elements. As with all Mississippian mortuary portraits, their faces are mask-like with half-open mouths, bared teeth, and staring eyes. The faces bear the residue of paint that probably indicated ritual tattoos or body paint denoting their rank.

Scholars have remarked on the similarities between the royal couple of Etowah and funerary portraits of the pharaoh and his queen found in Egyptian tombs. Perhaps the Etowah sculptures, and others like them, were also conceived as the repository of the departed spirits of the founding ancestors, for historic accounts indicate that the shrine figures were attended with utmost care by the temple priests. Indeed at least one of the mortuary figures found in Mound C was apparently interred in its own sarcophagus of limestone slabs.

Both of the marble figures from Etowah had been broken during the burial process. It would appear from the evidence that it may have been intentional, perhaps because of an enemy attack on the city. Brown writes, "Since this grave was associated with a burnt rubbish layer originating up-slope on the mound— perhaps from destruction of the summit structure by fire—there is reason to infer that a major disaster befell the Etowans, including the distinct possibility of profanement due to a defeat similar to that of the Mississippi River Capaha as related in the 1541 narratives of Hernando De Soto" (Brown 1985, 105). Brown is referring to the passage in the chronicles of Garcilaso de la Vega in which he tells of the looting of a mortuary temple by the enemies of the Capaha, the Casquins.

> The Casquins moved on to the temple in the large public plaza which was the burial place of all who had ever ruled that land—the fathers, grandfathers and other ancestors of the Capaha. The temples and sepulchres, as we have stated elsewhere, are the most venerated and esteemed sites among the natives. . . . Summoning all of their forces so that everyone might enjoy the triumph, the Casquins went to this temple and sepulchre, and since they realized how much Capaha . . . would resent their daring to enter and desecrate this place, they not only proceeded within but committed every infamy and affront they could. Sacking it of all ornaments and riches, they took the spoils and trophies which had been made from the losses of their own ancestors. Then they threw to the floor each of the wooden chests which served as sepulchers, and for their own satisfaction and vengeance as well as for an affront to their enemies, strewed upon the ground the very bones and bodies the chests enclosed. Afterward not content with having cast these remains to the ground, they trod upon them and kicked them with utter contempt and scorn. (Varner and Varner 1980, 438)

Lewis H. Larson, Jr., who was in charge of extensive excavations of the Etowah site, commented that "the site . . . was defined primarily by its defensive works, an encircling moat and bastioned palisade. That the town was stoutly and probably very securely defended argues that warfare was an omnipresent reality in the daily lives of the Etowah residents" (Galloway 1989, 134). James Brown calls Etowah "a classic stockaded town of the period" (Brown 1985, 94).

Located on the banks of the Etowah River, the town proper covers fifty-six acres and includes six mounds (see figure 56). The three largest mounds, A, B, and C, are grouped around a large plaza. A second plaza, paved with clay, lies to the east of Mound A. A ramp originally ran from the paved plaza to the summit of Mound A, which, like the other mounds, is a flat-topped pyramid (see plates 17–19). It is sixty-one feet high, and its base covers approximately three acres. The flat area on top of the mound is three-quarters the size of a football field and commands an impressive view of the surrounding plain. Neither Mound A nor the smaller Mound B has been excavated. However, Mound C, which stands on the west side of the plaza, has drawn extensive attention over the years, and it is the source of the wealth of artifacts that have made Etowah justifiably famous.

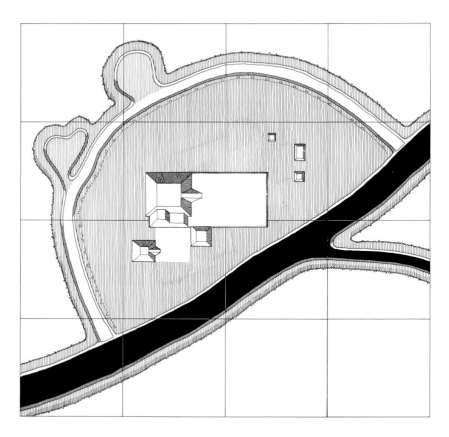

56. Etowah site, Cartersville, Georgia; Mississippian period, A.D. 1000–1450. From *Prehistoric Architecture in the Eastern United States* by William N. Morgan (Cambridge: The MIT Press, 1980).

Etowah first came to the attention of European settlers when the Reverend Elias Cornelius, traveling through northern Georgia in the company of eight Cherokees in 1817, came across the ruins. He asked his Indian guides about the origin of the mounds but reported that they had no reply except to say "they were never put up by our people" (Galloway 1989, 133). The first systematic study of the mounds was undertaken in 1873 by Charles C. Jones, Jr., who thought the Etowah site was the most remarkable mound group in the state.

It was not until 1884, however, that extensive archaeological excavations were begun by John P. Rogan under the direction of the Bureau of American Ethnology, Smithsonian Institution. Rogan concentrated his efforts on Mound C, which, although not the largest of the mounds, was estimated to be the likely site of the mortuary temple. He came across a total of eleven burials; they yielded a number of artifacts, including several embossed copper plates since known as the Rogan plates. One of these plates depicts a winged and masked dancer wearing a bellows-shaped apron, a beaded forelock, circular earrings, a bi-lobed arrow headdress, and a columella shell necklace. He carries a war club in one hand and a decapitated head in the other—probably a rattle in the form of a human head. This bird-man was at first thought to represent an eagle or a thunderbird. More recently, scholars have determined that the figure probably represents the falcon-impersonator, the hero or religious entity found throughout the Mississippian world.

Despite the interest aroused by Rogan's find, no further excavations were conducted until 1925, when Warren Moorehead began a three-year exploration of the Etowan site. He discovered a number of additional burials and also gained new insights into the extent of the village that surrounded the mounds. In 1953, the site was purchased by the Georgia Historical Commission and in the summer of that year new excavations were begun, headed by William Sears. The following summer, Lewis Larson joined the project with the intention of thoroughly examining the ruins of Mound C. After five years of intense effort, he discovered 210 additional burials, the foundations of eight buildings, and thousands of artifacts, many incorporating motifs associated with the Southeastern Ceremonial Complex. Larson writes, "The Cult objects appear to constitute elements of costume worn and objects carried or used during rituals. Many of these objects appear to have been parts of larger wholes that were not preserved in their entirety. For example, the sheet-copper symbol badges and the large sheet-copper plates with embossed Cult motifs were part of massive headdresses, many apparently with feathers. . . . Objects that were carried were invariably crafted to mimic weapons. Noncostume or nonweapon objects . . . included stone palettes, shell bowls . . . , carved wooden effigy rattles and effigy pipes." He goes on to say, "The recovery of the costume detail allows us to conclude with certainty that there were individuals who indeed dressed like the human and anthropomorphized bird figures portrayed on the shell gorgets and sheet-copper plates" (Galloway 1989, 140).

ABOUT 100 MILES southeast of Etowah, on the outskirts of the modern city of Macon, lie the ruins of yet another Mississippian town, which may be even older than Etowah. The first recorded mention of these ruins is found in an account given by one of General James Oglethorpe's rangers in 1739. He wrote, "We camped at Ocmulgas River where there are three Mounts raised by the Indians over three of their Great Kings who were killed in the Wars" (Mereness 1916, 200). In 1773, botanist and explorer William Bartram passed through the area and wrote, "About seventy or eighty miles above the confluence of the Oakmulge and Ocone, the trading path, from Augusta to the Creek nation, crosses these fine rivers, which are there forty miles apart. On the east banks of the Oakmulge, this trading road runs nearly two miles through ancient Indian fields, which are called the Oakmulge fields. . . . On the heights of these low grounds are yet visible monuments, or traces, of an ancient town, such as artificial mounts or terraces, squares and banks encircling considerable areas. Their old fields and planting lands extend up and down the river, fifteen or twenty miles from the site" (Bartram 1958, 52–53).

The "ancient town" to which Bartram refers was the result of an early penetration of Mississippian people into the central Georgia area. Its construction preceded that of Etowah by at least two centuries, but it appears to have been founded by a group of people who shared the Etowans' life-style and probably their religion as well. It is likely that the people who arrived at Ocmulgee around A.D. 980–1000 were part of the wave of immigrants that moved outward from the Cahokia region to bring the Mississippian way of life to less-organized peoples throughout the Southeast from the Yazoo Basin to the Cumberland Plateau. However, unlike the peaceful intrusion that characterized the Mississippians' arrival in Winterville, the Ocmulgee Mississippians appear to have invaded the Macon Plateau and driven out the earlier inhabitants, the Swift Creek people. Their culture was a variant of the Woodland period hunters and gatherers who engaged in marginal agricultural activities and built small burial mounds. The Swift Creek people had lived on the Macon Plateau for nearly 500 years, but evidence of their culture virtually disappeared from the area with the arrival of the Mississippians.

Charles Fairbanks, who compiled a comprehensive report on the Ocmulgee site for the National Park Service, wrote, "The Macon Plateau period is probably the best example in the Southeast of an invasion by one group into territory previously occupied by another. There is no evidence of the development of any traits in the Macon Plateau focus out of the earlier patterns found in central Georgia. It is a sharp break in the cultural sequence. . . . I suspect the newcomers actually drove out the Swift Creek inhabitants" (Fairbanks 1956, 42). He goes on to say that shortly after their arrival, the invaders established a ceremonial center on the Ocmulgee site (see figure 57). They built log tombs and buried a number of important individuals. Soon after the burials a mound was erected over the graves. Fairbanks writes, "It was a flat-topped mound and seems to have had some sort of temple on its summit. Burials were made in and around the mound, and as each mound stage was added it continued to be used as the burial center for the community. . . . The evidence of bone cleaning and complicated interments is sufficient to postulate elaborate rituals accompanying these operations" (Fairbanks 1956, 42) (see plates 20 and 21).

Although excavations of the Ocmulgee site failed to yield the same sort of spectacular Southern Cult objects recovered from Etowah, Spiro, or Moundville, cult-related objects found at Ocmulgee included ceramic effigy pots, conch shell drinking cups, ritual axes or celts, and a ritually preserved cougar jawbone.

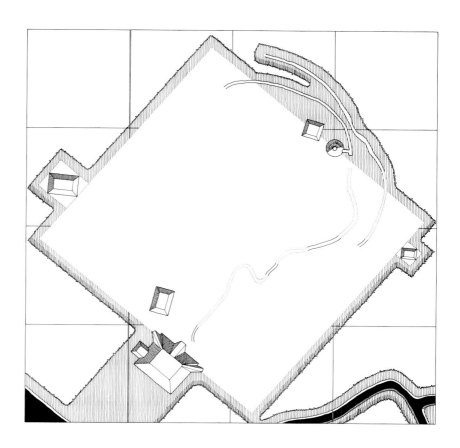

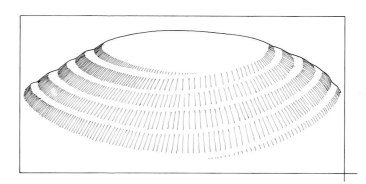

57. Ocmulgee site, Macon, Georgia; Mississippian period, A.D. 1000–1200. From *Prehistoric Architecture in the Eastern United States* by William N. Morgan (Cambridge: The MIT Press, 1980).

Perhaps the most intriguing archaeological feature at the site was found in the floor of one of the temples. Located on the west side of the lodge between the wall and the central fire pit is a raised platform in the shape of a bird. Enough of the surface features of the effigy remained to enable archaeologists to confirm a forked-eye design around the eye and a "scalloped effect across the shoulders," probably representing feathers (Pope 1956, 31). This unique feature has been preserved as part of the reconstruction of the site which has, since 1936, been under the jurisdiction of the National Park Service.

It is not clear what happened to the Mississippian people who built Ocmulgee. Their occupation of the town only lasted about 200 years, after which the site lay vacant for over two centuries. By the time the temple mounds of Etowah were under construction, those of Ocmulgee were already deserted and crumbling. "We do not know . . . whether the last occupants left here in a body to settle elsewhere, whether they gradually died off, whether they were finally exterminated by neighbors who had themselves developed large settled communities capable of effective military action. Other ideas came to Georgia from the Mississippi Valley, but Ocmulgee lay silent and was passed by" (Pope 1956, 39).

A number of the traits practiced by the Ocmulgee people did, however, continue elsewhere in the area as subsequent waves of Mississippian influence inundated the Southeast. The two most distinctive Mississippian traits—intensive agriculture and ceremonial mound-building and accompanying religious beliefs—found wide acceptance throughout the region. Mississippian ideas were incorporated into the old Woodland ways, and the resultant hybrid cultures proved durable and adaptive. Successful farming led to population growth, which led to more elaborate social and ideological structures and a proliferation of art forms. In Georgia, this trend reached a peak during the thirteenth and fourteenth centuries, the high point of the Etowah culture. In middle Tennessee, temple mound sites were built along the valley of the Cumberland River. In eastern Tennessee, towns such as the large settlement on Hiwassee Island, at the confluence of the Hiwassee and Tennessee rivers, flourished for several hundred years, beginning in the twelfth century. Many of these towns reflect the interaction that took place between the Woodland people and the Mississippian immigrants, including the growth of the Southeastern Ceremonial Complex and the modification of existing art forms into those reflecting Mississippian techniques and ideas.

Then for several centuries, until the arrival of the European invaders, there was a period of slow decline. Mississippian practices continued to be followed but without the same enthusiasm and vigor that characterized earlier phases. Both the Lamar culture in Georgia and Florida and the Dallas culture in Tennessee and the Carolinas are examples of the late phase of Mississippian development. Both cultures are a mix of Mississippian patterns and indigenous Woodland cultures. Population continued to increase as local groups were absorbed into the agricultural life-style, but there was a watering down of the most salient aspects of Mississippian cultural patterns and a calcification of creative energies.

Shell art, especially the decorations found on shell gorgets, is a useful means of tracing stylistic and technical developments during the period of Mississippian infiltration (see plate 22). Gorgets appear to have been an important element of high-status costumes and are sometimes depicted in Mississippian art in conjunction with mythic figures. They have been found over a wide geographic area from the Mississippi Valley eastward to the Appalachian region and south to the Gulf Coast. Stylistically, they range from the lively naturalism found at Spiro and elsewhere in the Mississippi Valley to the almost totally abstract examples from Tennessee. Generally, the earlier examples are more naturalistic and more closely resemble the classic style of the Mississippi Valley, while the later examples, such as those associated with the Citico site in Tennessee, are more stylized, with natural subjects reduced to bands of geometric decoration (see figure 58). While many of the latter are quite beautiful, they lack the spontaneity and immediacy of the earlier figurative pieces.

The circular format lends itself to symmetrical compositions, so it is not surprising that a number of shell gorgets exhibit paired images. The cross-and-circle motif, possibly symbolizing the sun or the four cardinal points, is an obvious choice for the circular format, and the scalloped triskle, in which concentric circles surround three radiating whorls, is another. Mirror images of dancers and birds, often turkeys, are also frequently represented. Conventionalized human figures are a relatively late development in the area of shell gorget decoration (see plate 22).

The Late Mississippian period was a time of adaptation and acculturation throughout the Southeast. The wave-like effect of infiltration from the heartland produced increasingly hybrid variations of cultures based ever more loosely on Mississippian prototypes. The Native Americans of the historic period were the inheritors of this amalgam of Woodland and Mississippian traditions. An interesting example of a town from the late period is found in Montgomery County, North Carolina, on the banks of the Little Pee Dee River. It is known today as Town Creek.

Town Creek was used as a ceremonial center from around A.D. 1450 to 1650 by a group of Indians known as the Pee Dee people (see figure 59). It is thought that the Pee Dee people were related to the historic Creeks, who were influenced by the Lamar culture of the Macon Plateau, according to Joeffrey L.

58. Shell gorget showing rattlesnake motif, Roane County, Tennessee; Mississippian period, A.D. 1200–1400. Courtesy of the Frank H. McClung Museum, University of Tennessee, Knoxville.

Coe of the University of North Carolina, director of site excavation. Much of Coe's restoration of the Town Creek site was derived from Creek customs and traditions.

The Creeks, one of the Muskhogean-speaking peoples of the Southeast, were traditionally called the People of One Fire. The name Creeks came from Ocheese Creek, the English traders' name for the Ocmulgee River in Georgia, where a number of Muskhogean people lived. The Creek Confederacy was the largest of all precontact intertribal alliances. Its strength lay in the artful diplomacy of the Creeks in incorporating alien tribes of different cultures into their alliance.

The social and political framework of the confederacy had three strong supports—the clan, the *talwa*, and the fires. Creek clans were extended families who considered themselves related through a common ancestor. Relationships were traced through the mother's side, and all children became members of their mother's clan. A person could not marry anyone who was a member of the same clan. There were at least nine clans within the tribes that formed the Creek Confederacy, and the relationships among them formed the basis for a strong network that strengthened the confederacy as a whole.

The word *talwa* meant "town" in the Muskhogean language, but the concept of the talwa exceeded our meaning of the word town as a geographic place. The talwa was actually a tribal territorial province that included a ceremonial center and a number of smaller villages associated with it. Some of the larger talwas, such as the chiefdom of Coosa mentioned in the de Soto chronicles, held sway over large areas that extended several hundred miles and included numerous villages. Each talwa could be identified by a special emblem, such as an eagle, serpent, or fish. These emblems were represented as sculptures, on pipes, in copper and other media, including the distinctive designs that a talwa's warriors used in body and face painting and tattooing. The word talwa also meant the spirit of the town, often represented by a special individual who lived in the temple complex.

The "fires," the third element of the confederacy, divided the talwas into two groups: the "peace towns," known as white fire, and the "war towns," known as red. White towns were places of refuge where peace treaties were consummated and where sanctuary could be requested. At red towns, war was declared and enemies were executed. Red and white towns played against each other in the ball games. But despite the apparent opposition of the red and white talwas, the members of each of these groups called themselves the "people of one fire" because they came together to celebrate the Busk and to renew their common bonds (Lewis and Kneberg 1958, 95).

"The red and white fires," writes Lewis, "with their contrasting but balanced peace and war functions, accomplished more than the uniting of the talwas; they were basic factors in the political operation and growth of the confederacy. For example, when alien tribes were incorporated, they usually joined the white fire. Thus, the talwas furnished the ceremonial and administrative units, the clans provided the personal bonds between individuals, and the fires cemented both into the strong political fabric of the great confederation" (Lewis and Kneberg 1958, 96).

The Town Creek reconstruction of buildings includes a thatched-roof temple atop a platform mound (see plates 23–27). The interior of the temple is covered with murals, a hypothetical reconstruction of interior wall decoration used by the Pee Dee people. A circular mortuary house, with a depiction of a funeral ceremony, is located near the platform mound. At the base of the

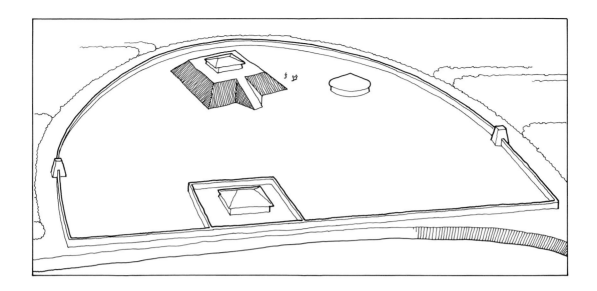

59. Town Creek site, Mt.
Gilead, North Carolina; Late
Mississippian period, A.D.
1450–1600. From *Prehistoric
Architecture in the Eastern
United States* by William N.
Morgan (Cambridge: The
MIT Press, 1980).

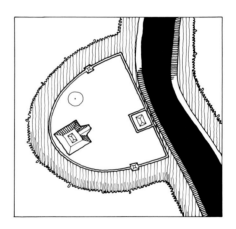

ramp that leads up to the temple is the square ground (a plaza or community commons), and adjacent to that is a game pole topped with the skull of a bear. Surrounding these structures is a palisade with two gates. Four sets of palisades originally guarded any access to the ceremonial center. It is clear from excavations that Town Creek was strictly for ceremonial and not for residential use.

Town Creek and other Mississippian settlements in the coastal region of the Carolinas represent the easternmost fringes of Mississippian influence, and therefore can be viewed as peripheral to the development of Mississippian culture (see plate 28). However, provincial though they may have been, they do indicate the vast scope of Mississippian influence in the Southeast. The wonderfully vibrant and complex culture that had its first stirrings in the American Bottoms and the Mississippi Valley had enough ideological and technological punch to send its influence all the way to the shores of the Atlantic Ocean and to spread its agricultural life-style and rich mythology over thousands of miles, from the Great Lakes to the Gulf of Mexico. Even the Florida Peninsula, at the farthest frontier of Mississippian influence, echoed the message of the Moundbuilders, although among the ancient Floridians only the Apalachee of the Panhandle region seriously pursued the Mississippians' agricultural interests. It is one of the interesting ironies of fate that Florida, the least Mississippianized region of the Moundbuilders' domain, was to be the point of contact with those who would forever destroy the remnants of that ancient civilization.

CHAPTER 7

La Florida

In time, Three Black Doves will come from the East, from across the Great Water, to die and to be buried here in the Center of the Earth. Their seed will sink deep into our Sacred Soil, into our wellsprings, corrupting our waters, our forests, our creatures, our sons. The Three Black Doves will pass on their fear of Mother Earth to the tribe that will spring up from their seeds. Lightning, Rainbow, Night will be lost. When, after much time and inglorious battle, all is out of harmony and the Great Spirit's work is destroyed, the Tequesta's World Below the Sky will end.

CREATION AND THE END OF THE
WORLD BELOW THE SKY
TEQUESTA LEGEND

WITHIN THE SOUTHEAST, Florida has always been a region with its own special flavor and style. Geographically, it is detached from the rest of the country, a jutting peninsula that often seems more island than mainland. This physical isolation from the rest of the United States, plus its proximity to the Caribbean, may account for the distinctive traits that developed in Florida and made it unique in the fabric of Mississippian cultural patterns.

Linguistically and culturally, Florida presents a bewildering array of possibilities (see map 3). It seems to operate outside the usual rules, with various traits refusing to line up in neat categories. Were the people of Crystal River Hopewellians or Mississippians? Were they in contact, via the Gulf of Mexico, with the great civilizations of Mexico, or did they independently invent platform mounds guarded by stone stelae? If the Safety Harbor people were Mississippian, why didn't they plant corn? How could they have participated in a religion based on an agricultural life-style if they weren't agriculturalists? Were the Key Marco people a late variant of the Mississippian tradition, or were their main contacts the Caribbean cultures with whom they obviously traded? And why are the copper objects discovered at Mount Royal, a prehistoric site on the St. Johns River in east-central Florida, nearly identical with copper objects found at the Spiro site in Oklahoma?

Mount Royal, located near present-day Palatka on the east side of the St. Johns River, provides an interesting example of the kind of hybridized Mississippianism that flourished in Florida during the precontact period (see figures 60 and 61). The St. Johns culture had a long history in the region, dating back to at least 500 B.C. During that time, certain patterns were established that gave the culture a stable base, which was elaborated upon during subsequent periods of development. Since the region is rich in natural resources, the population continued to rely largely on hunting and gathering even after corn agriculture was introduced sometime after A.D. 100. Great piles of oyster shells confirm the importance of shellfish in the diet of the St. Johns

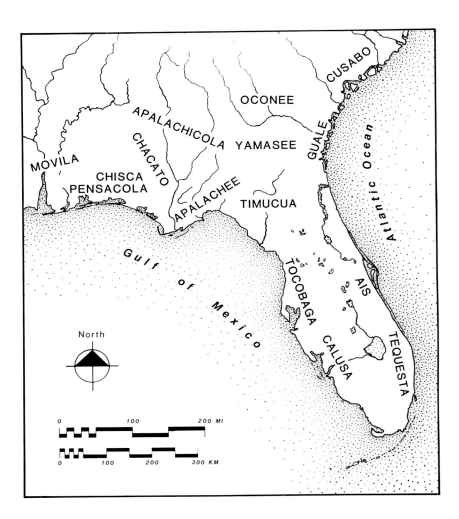

MAP 3. Indian groups
in Florida at the time
of European contact.
Courtesy of the Florida
Department of State,
Division of Historical
Resources.

people. Although permanent villages were first established at about the same
time as the introduction of horticulture, much of the population continued to
move seasonally from the river to the coast in order to take advantage of the
resources of the coastal strand.

Much of our knowledge of the religious practices of the St. Johns people
is a result of the excavations of Clarence Moore, who visited the area in the
late 1890s. Originally part of the Hopewellian tradition, burial rituals became
increasingly complex as new influences entered the area. Whereas it appears
that all members of the group prior to A.D. 100 enjoyed the same treatment
after death—secondary burial in mounds—later burials indicate that only
high-status individuals and their families were given such preference. Grave
offerings also became more elaborate, often including copper disks, decorated

animal jaws, bird-effigy pipes, and shell drinking cups. Ceremonialism of the period after A.D. 1200 is characterized by the adoption of a variety of Mississippian traits. Several ceremonial mounds, similar to those found elsewhere in the Southeast, were excavated by Moore in the mid-1890s. Among them was Mount Royal.

William Bartram, who had visited the Mount Royal site in the late 1700s, described it like this: "At about fifty yards distance from the landing place, stands a magnificent Indian mount. . . . But what greatly contributed towards completing the magnificence of the scene, was a noble Indian highway, which led from the great mount, on a straight line, three quarters of a mile, first through a point or wing of the orange grove, and continuing thence through an awful forest of live oaks, it was terminated by palms and laurel magnolias, on the verge of an oblong artificial lake, which was on the edge of an extensive green savanna. This grand highway was about fifty yards wide, sunk a little below the common level, and the earth thrown up on each side, making a bank about two feet high. Neither nature nor art could any where present a more striking contrast, as you approached this savanna" (Bartram 1958, 101–2).

60. Mount Royal site, Putnam County, Florida; Mississippian period, A.D. 800–1500. From *Prehistoric Architecture in the Eastern United States* by William N. Morgan (Cambridge: The MIT Press, 1980).

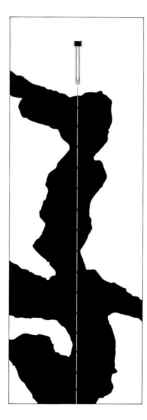
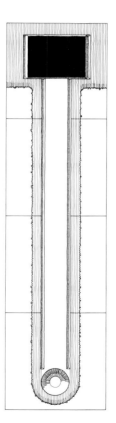

61. The Mount Royal site on the St. Johns River, Putnam County, Florida. Photo by Barbara Gibbs.

The Mount Royal mound was about 16 feet high and 550 feet in diameter when it was visited by Moore in 1893–94. It was built with earth taken from a barrow pit about three-quarters of a mile away, creating the artificial lake mentioned by Bartram. The lake and the mound were connected by a sunken causeway nearly 2,600 feet long. This unusual feature is similar to artificial ridges and ponds constructed by Woodland period people in the Lake Okeechobee area 200 miles to the south. Artifacts recovered from the mound by Moore included Busycon shells, stone celts, a variety of unique ceremonial vessels, and a copper plate displaying the Southern Cult forked-eye motif. The plate is so similar to a copper plate recovered from the Spiro site that it is tempting to argue that they could have been made by the same artist. That possibility is not as far-fetched as it sounds, since a variety of other copper and bead artifacts from Mount Royal were obviously acquired through the extensive trade network that operated throughout the Southeast beginning in Woodland times.

The Thursby site, not far downriver from Mount Royal, was also excavated by Moore. It yielded a large variety of uniquely shaped ceramic vessels, similar to those found at Mount Royal, as well as a cache of effigy figurines. Some forty-eight different animals, including Florida panthers, bears, squirrels, turkeys, fishes, and turtles, were represented among the figurines, along with evidence of several varieties of plants, such as acorns, gourds, and corncobs. Although small ceramic figures have been found occasionally elsewhere they are rare, and the Florida group is unique in terms of variety and style.

One other interesting feature of the region was discovered when a dragline operator pulled a large wooden totem out of the St. Johns River near the Thursby site in 1955 (see figure 62). The totem, probably a charnel house guardian and not a clan totem such as is found in the Pacific Northwest, represents a horned owl. It is over six feet tall and evidently was originally stuck in the ground, since the bottom of the pole has rotted away. A radiocarbon date of A.D. 1300 was obtained from a sample of the carving (Milanich and Fairbanks 1980, 166). The only place where similarly large carvings have been discovered is the Lake Okeechobee Basin of south-central Florida, where they were apparently associated with mortuary activities.

The most typically Mississippian site in Florida is, not surprisingly, found in the far-north region of the state, near present-day Tallahassee. Located within 100 miles of several major Weeden Island period sites, including Kolomoki, the Lake Jackson site represents the largest known ceremonial center in northern Florida; it is associated with the Fort Walton culture, a Florida variation of the Mississippian cultural pattern.

According to University of Florida archaeologist Jerald Milanich, there is no doubt that the Apalachee Indians encountered by the Narváez and de Soto expeditions in the mid-1500s were the remnants of the Fort Walton people. European materials have been found in several Fort Walton sites, and the main ceremonial center on the shores of Lake Jackson was probably the town that de Soto called "Apalachee" (Milanich and Fairbanks 1980, 193).

Until the mid-1970s, many scholars believed that the Fort Walton people were Mississippian immigrants who had moved into the Florida Panhandle sometime after A.D. 1300. Similarities between Fort Walton ceramic vessels and those found at Moundville in Alabama suggested either a close affiliation with the Alabama Mississippians or even a migration of Moundville "refugees" to the area of northwest Florida (see plate 29). More recent evidence points instead to the indigenous development of the Fort Walton culture out of the earlier Weeden Island complex. "Quite likely," writes Milanich, "contact down the Chattahoochee River with other emerging Mississippian peoples in the Southeast brought new ideas to the late Weeden Island people, ideas for organizing increasingly larger societies and ideas for more intensive and efficient agriculture. Fort Walton therefore represents the 'Mississippianization' of Weeden Island society" (Milanich and Fairbanks 1980, 194).

The political and social structure of the Fort Walton people echoes that of Mississippian cultures throughout the Southeast. Lake Jackson, with its array of mounds, a plaza, remnants of a good-sized village, and evidence of Mississippian ceremonial practices, probably functioned as the "capital city" of the region (see figure 63). The ceremonial complex originally included six mounds and covered an area of about sixty-six acres. The largest of the mounds is

62. Owl-effigy, wood, St. Johns River, Putnam County, Florida; Mississippian period, A.D. 1100–1300. Courtesy of the Florida Museum of Natural History, Gainesville.

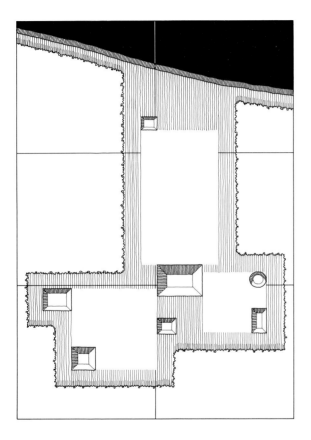

63. Lake Jackson site, Leon County, Florida; Late Mississippian period, A.D. 1300–1600. From *Prehistoric Architecture in the Eastern United States* by William N. Morgan (Cambridge: The MIT Press, 1980).

about twenty-five feet high and has a ramp that leads up the east side. Calvin Jones, of the Division of Archives, History and Records Management in Tallahassee, directed the excavation of one of the mounds and discovered a series of clay layers that apparently served as the floors for successive structures built on the top of the mound. The graves of chiefs, family members, and other high-status individuals were located in the mound along with the remains of apparent sacrificial victims, trophy skulls, and the bundled bones of ancestors.

Several copper breastplates were retrieved from Mound 3 of the Lake Jackson site during Jones's excavation. They were carved to represent dancers dressed in bird costumes, perhaps supernatural beings or mythic ancestors. Repoussé copper breastplates similar to these were recovered from the Etowah site in northern Georgia and the Spiro site in eastern Oklahoma. It is thought that these skillfully worked copper objects may have been produced in special workshops at some of the major Mississippian sites farther to the north and brought to Florida as trade items for the local leaders and their families.

A long-nosed bird dancer was represented on one of the breastplates found in Mound 3 (see figure 64). Part of a magnificent costume worn by the high-ranking woman interred in the mound, the dancer is depicted wearing special moccasins, a beaded belt with a long sash, a bellows-shaped apron, a necklace of shell beads, and a feathered cape. In one hand the dancer carries a mace, symbol of authority, and in the other a severed head. The figure's shoulders are decorated with concentric circles, and she wears a headdress featuring both the bi-lobed arrow and the circular sun shield, with an ogee symbolizing the sun's eternally open eye. The figure's long, hooked nose recalls the Long-Nosed God found in Mississippian iconography throughout the Southeast. A second breastplate found in Mound 3 also depicts a dancing figure wearing a feathered cape and carrying a ceremonial club (see figure 65).

The other two copper plates found in Mound 3 were not originally attached but were too fragile to be separated after being excavated. One of these plates represents an elder bird-man, possibly a revered ancestor lying in state. This figure wears an elaborate feathered headdress, and his face is decorated with intricate designs. The closed wings of his cloak may imply the motionless state of death compared with the open wings of the dancing figures. The plate found in conjunction with the bird-man depicts a falcon without any anthropomorphic features. Like the dead bird-man, the falcon is frontally displayed. An interesting feature is the extruded tongue, which is also found in numerous Mississippian figures in a mortuary context.

The Lake Jackson site apparently functioned as a ceremonial center beginning around A.D. 1000. The mounds were built over a period of several centuries, and there is evidence of substantial residential habitation both near the mounds and in the surrounding area. For reasons that remain unclear, the site was abandoned sometime in the early 1500s and was apparently no longer in use as a ceremonial center by the time Hernando de Soto visited there in 1539. Its reputation was still legendary, however, for the Apalachee, the inheritors of the Fort Walton tradition, were spoken of with awe by the Tampa Bay Indians, who told de Soto stories of their great wealth and power.

Today, forty-one acres of the mound complex and village area are incorporated into the Lake Jackson State Archaeological Site, administered by

64. Drawing of a hawk dancer from a repoussé copper breastplate, Lake Jackson site, Leon County, Florida. Drawing by Calvin Jones. Courtesy of the Florida Division of Historical Resources, Tallahassee.

65. Rubbing of a dancing figure from a copper breastplate, Lake Jackson site, Leon County, Florida; Mississippian period, A.D. 1300–1600. Courtesy of the Florida Division of Natural Resources, Tallahassee.

the Florida Department of Natural Resources. Footpaths lead between the mounds, and kudzu vines hang in luxurious blankets from the live oaks and pines. In the distance, the lake shines in the Florida sun, and the staccato rapping of the woodpecker breaks the silence that long ago settled over Florida's first capital city.

SEVERAL HUNDRED MILES south of Lake Jackson, in what is now called the Tampa Bay area, another Mississippianized culture formed around A.D. 1000. It is known as the Safety Harbor culture, after the type site on Tampa Bay. Villages similar to those of the Mississippian people were constructed along the Gulf Coast from Tarpon Springs south to the Sarasota region. Most of these towns had a single, large temple mound, which was periodically rebuilt. A ramp usually extended down from the top of the mound to a plaza. The village living area surrounded the plaza. Burial mounds were usually located nearby.

Safety Harbor mound-village complexes probably functioned as small chiefdoms. From Spanish accounts we know that at certain times two or more of these town-chiefdoms were allied, and one chief held the others as vassals, receiving tribute from their villages. The Safety Harbor people, in contrast to most Mississippianized societies, never practiced agriculture. Perhaps the combination of sandy soil and the abundant natural resources of the region made agriculture unprofitable and unnecessary. The Safety Harbor people instead appear to represent a Fort Walton–influenced elaboration on the basic Weeden Island coastal life-style. Mississippian ideas concerning political and social organization seem to have infiltrated the area, but other ideas, such as Mississippian religious concepts based on agriculture, may have been unsuited to the experiences of the local people.

However, excavations of several Safety Harbor sites have provided evidence of burial practices similar to those found at other Mississippian sites, including the presence of bundles of bones that were stored in the village charnel house prior to interment. Juan Ortiz, a young Spaniard who had accompanied the Narváez expedition to Florida in 1528, was captured by the Indians of the Tampa Bay area and lived among them for nearly ten years until he was rescued by de Soto. As he described it, his life among the Indians had included being made to guard a temple that contained the bodies of the dead. Garcilaso de la Vega, who chronicled the de Soto expedition, also mentions a temple containing wooden boxes that served as tombs (Varner and Varner 1980, 65–66).

There may have been close connections between the Safety Harbor people and the Mississippianized Fort Walton culture of the Florida Panhandle. The connection is suggested by a remarkable bowl from north Florida now in the collection of the Indian Temple Mound Museum in Fort Walton Beach (see plate 30). One side of the bowl has designs typical of the Fort Walton style of ceramic decoration, while the other side is covered with designs found on Safety Harbor pottery from the Tampa Bay region. Perhaps this hybrid piece marked an important alliance between the two areas—an interdynastic marriage or maybe a peace treaty (Steven Tuthill, personal communication).

Today, the Safety Harbor site lies within Philippe Park overlooking the west shore of Old Tampa Bay (see figure 66 and plate 31). Maintained by the Pinellas County Park Department, the site has been landscaped with a series of retaining walls to combat shoreline erosion. The site originally included a platform mound, a plaza, a burial mound, and an associated village area. Matthew Stirling conducted the first excavations of the site in 1929, uncovering more than 100 burials along with a number of ceramic vessels. Additional excavations were undertaken in 1948 by Ripley Bullen and John Griffin.

Today, only the platform mound is visible. Its incorporation into the neatly landscaped park makes it difficult to imagine the layout of the town. Still, if you stand on top of the mound and look out over the bay, it is possible to imagine the original beauty of the site and to see the significance of the confrontation that took place here nearly 500 years ago. It was at Tampa Bay that Panfilo de Narváez landed in 1528 to launch the first major overland expedition into Florida. Within 200 years the indigenous population had been decimated by warfare and European diseases.

The relationship between Mississippian culture and the ancient peoples of south Florida has long been a subject for debate. In terms of population

66. Safety Harbor mounds, Hillsborough County, Florida. Photo by Barbara Gibbs.

size, political importance, and social organization, the Calusa were the most significant groups of Indians in south Florida at the time of European intrusion, and they were probably the first to have contact with the Spanish. Juan Ponce de León, who first ventured into Florida in 1513, apparently made contact with the Calusa somewhere on the Gulf Coast south of Fort Myers. That the Calusa shared a number of traits with their Mississippian contemporaries to the north has been documented since the middle sixteenth century, when Pedro Menéndez established a fort and settlement close to the Calusa town of Calos near present-day Fort Myers. From Spanish accounts and archaeological evidence, we can determine that the city of Calos probably had a population of around 1,000, with 5,000 to 6,000 associated individuals in the immediate vicinity. It is estimated that another 5,000 to 10,000 people living in the inland areas were also under Calusa control. The Spaniards reported that this vast Calusa domain, which extended from Florida's west coast eastward into the Okeechobee Basin, was ruled by a single chief whom they called El Rey, the king. According to the accounts of a young Spaniard named Fontaneda who lived among the Calusa for seventeen years, this chief ruled over at least fifty villages, and tribute was brought to him from throughout his empire.

The capital city of King Calos is thought to have been located on Mound Key in Estero Bay near Fort Myers Beach. Mound Key is a small, roughly circular island crosscut with Indian-built canals and capped with several large artificial mounds built of earth and shell, which served as platforms for civic and ceremonial structures (see figure 67). The presence of extensive shell middens implies a long period of occupation by the Indians. Like the Safety

67. Shell mound at Calos in Estero Bay, Lee County, Florida. Photo by Barbara Gibbs.

Harbor people to the north, the Calusa were not interested in agriculture. Hunting and fishing appear to have provided the mainstay of their diet.

Frank Cushing, in the 1890s, explored the remnants of a Calusa town located on Marco Island and was the first to suggest a connection between the Calusa and the great Mississippian civilization to the north. He saw a distinct similarity between the artifacts he had excavated from the "court of the pile dwellers" at Key Marco and those that had been recently found at the Etowah site in northern Georgia. Later scholars agreed that definite similarities could be documented, but Key Marco was no Lake Jackson. The close relationships evident between the Fort Walton people of the Florida Panhandle and the Mississippian cultures found in Georgia and Alabama were lacking in Calusa examples. Recent interpretations based on available evidence suggest that while there were some ties through trade between the Calusa and the Mississippianized Indians to the north, the Indians of south Florida developed a distinctively different culture. An essay by Randolph J. Widmer, presented at the 1984 Cottonlandia Conference in Greenwood, Mississippi, sums up the prevailing view of the Mississippian–South Florida connection as follows:

> What we see then in south Florida is a distinct ceremonial complex, perhaps best termed the South Florida Ceremonial Complex, maintaining a distinct regional and artifactual expression ultimately derived from a common pan-eastern Hopewellian-based ceremonial complex, but incorporating various Southeastern Ceremonial Complex motifs and traits into an indigenous religious system. Other than the Black Drink ceremony, which is common to both ceremonial complexes, there appears to be little similarity in ceremonies. The deities in south Florida are more naturalistic than those in the Southeastern Ceremonial Complex and do not mix human and animal forms. This is thought to be due to the difference in subsistence patterns between the two groups [the people of south Florida remained basically hunter and gatherers and never practiced extensive agriculture], which results in the development of two distinct ceremonial and religious systems. Yet because the two areas have similar levels of socio-cultural integration and are derived from a common Hopewellian ceremonial complex, many of the traits and characteristics are similar. The South Florida Ceremonial Complex can be historically traced up through the seventeenth century, probably originating at approximately A.D. 700–800. This is the time when chiefdoms first appear on the southwest Florida coast and provide the socio-political context for the development of an esoteric religious complex or cult. (Widmer 1989, 180)

The development of a distinctive south Florida cultural pattern was not the result of a lack of interaction between the Calusa and their Mississippian neighbors to the north. We know from Spanish accounts that the Calusa were trading with the Apalachees, the inheritors of the Mississippianized Fort Walton tradition, and pottery from the Safety Harbor area has been found at a number of sites in the south Florida area. The Calusa also built mounds and, like their Mississippian counterparts, constructed temples on the flat tops of these artificial mountains. However, in contrast to the Mississippian pattern, these temples do not seem to have been associated with mortuary functions. Instead, they seem to have served as repositories for ceremonial objects used in festivals and processions. This difference may help account for the general lack in Calusan art of themes associated with death and sacrifice. Instead of skulls, bones, and fantastic monsters, Calusan artists preferred to portray living animals, frequently in a most naturalistic way.

Naturalistic animal representations have a long history in south Florida, dating back at least to Hopewellian times. Widmer writes, "In south Florida these animal deities and representations retain their esoteric status from previous Hopewellian times. . . . Thus a continuation and elaboration of a broad animal-based pantheon develops, restricted from the general public in an esoteric religious context. . . . In the core Mississippian area these animal deities were replaced by god-animal deities [and human-animal combinations] and their attendant ceremonies, obviously related to the shift to full maize agriculture" (Galloway 1989, 176).

Some of the most beautiful examples of Calusan artistry come from the Key Marco site, a Calusa town that continued into the historic period. Cushing's excavations of the town uncovered a number of wood carvings that had been preserved because they were buried in the mud when the town was hastily abandoned sometime in the latter part of the eleventh century. Whether the residents left because of a natural disaster, such as a hurricane, or were driven out by unfriendly visitors has not been determined. There is evidence that many of the structures in the town were burned, and the artifacts were found scattered about as though they had been left behind during a quick retreat. Although the wooden artifacts had been well preserved by the thick muck which covered them for over 900 years, most did not survive the excavation process despite Cushing's best efforts to protect them. Once exposed to the air, the wood began almost at once to dry and split, so that only badly scarred remnants are extant today.

The masks, tablets, and sculptures recovered from the site were carved from several kinds of wood, including cypress, pine, and mangrove. Shell and stone tools were used along with shark-tooth adzes. Many of the surfaces of the artifacts were finely finished, indicating a sophisticated polishing technique. Many were also painted. Altogether, the objects hint at what must have been a fine wood-carving tradition that was probably widespread throughout the Southeast. One of the most spectacular objects found by Cushing was an elegant, small sculpture of a cat or a human costumed as a cat or panther (see plate 32). "Although it is barely six inches in height," Cushing wrote, "its dignity of pose may fairly be termed heroic and its . . . lines are to the last degree masterly" (Gilliland 1975, 116). Marion Gilliland, whose book *The Material Culture of Key Marco, Florida* provides a comprehensive study of the Key Marco artifacts, writes, "This specimen resembles more closely ancient Egyptian or Babylonian art than any other specimen so far found in America" (Gilliland 1975, 116).

Similarly, the roughly life-sized head of a pelican, which was found along with fragments of wing pieces, testifies to the artist's masterful handling of both the subject and the media (see figure 68). Other sculptures represent a variety of animals, including wolves, alligators, turtles, and deer. A finely carved life-sized sculpture of a beaked sea turtle was originally painted in black, white, and red (see figure 69). The eyes are carved so that they project outward from the head. An equally beautiful specimen is a representation of a deer head with separately articulated ears (see figure 70). This may well have been a mask or part of a costume used in a ceremony. It brings to mind the kinetic sculptures used in the ceremonies of the Eskimo and Northwest Coast peoples, although the high degree of naturalism is unique.

68. Pelican head, wood, Key Marco site, Marco Island, Florida; Mississippian period, A.D. 1000–1400. Courtesy of the Florida Museum of Natural History, Gainesville.

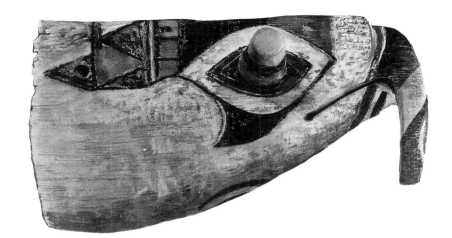

69. Sea turtle head,
wood, Key Marco site,
Marco Island, Florida;
Mississippian period,
A.D. 1000–1400.
National Museum
of Natural History,
Smithsonian Institution,
Washington, D.C.

70. Deer head with
articulated ears, wood,
Key Marco site, Collier
County, Florida; Calusa
culture, A.D. 1000–1400.
Courtesy of the Florida
Museum of Natural
History, Gainesville.

A number of other masks were discovered at the site. Several represent human-like forms, possibly heroic or mythological beings. A few portray animals, such as a cat-like figure originally painted with striped designs in blue, white, and black (see plate 32). Frequently, the features of the creature have been purposefully distorted—noses elongated, mouths twisted, eyes exaggerated. Most masks were painted with stripes, triangles, or circles. Some were inlaid with shell.

Unfortunately, most of the masks have disintegrated almost entirely. They were, however, recorded at the time of excavation by the artist Wells Sawyer, who accompanied the Cushing expedition. Sawyer's watercolors provide a vibrant record of these elaborate and mysterious objects and allow us to consider them in the context of other historic period works (Gilliland 1989).

The Key Marco site was destroyed by construction activities in the early twentieth century. However, it is still possible to visit the nearby Mound Key, where the ruins of Calos are located. Access to the island is by water via the Estero River. The site's condition is primitive, and there are no interpretative or other facilities on the island. The State of Florida manages the site but does not provide transportation or guides, so all arrangements must be made through private parties. The artificial shell island is entirely surrounded by dense mangrove swamps and is often plagued by swarms of mosquitoes, so a visit is not an adventure for the fainthearted. It is fascinating, however, to climb up the mountains of shell and to see the remains of the canals that provided the prehistoric Indians with access to the bay. Wildlife abounds on the island, and the abundant population of rare butterflies has attracted the attention of entomologists nationwide.

Like the other Indian cultures encountered by the Spanish, the Calusa, despite their large population and sophisticated social and political organization, did not long survive. Although they resisted steadfastly for more than a century, epidemics of European diseases and continual warfare depleted their resources. Like the other Indians of La Florida, the Calusa vanished into history.

It is difficult to imagine what would have happened to the Mississippian cultures of the Southeast had the Spaniards not arrived when they did. While it is true that the Mississippian tradition that had flourished in the American Bottoms had long since withered in the region of its birth, hybridized Mississippian cultures, such as those in Florida, were alive and well at the time of first contact with the European invaders. The earliest Spanish accounts described the Indians as "exceedingly tall and handsome" and suggested that many of them lived to be old (Milanich and Milbrath 1989, 189). The earliest images of the Indians, created by European artists such as Jacques Le Moyne, depict tall, muscular men and graceful, long-haired women dressed in exotic costumes, covered with decorative tattoos or body paint, and wearing strings of beads. Writes art historian Susan Milbrath, "Artists incorporated subtle references to the Garden of Eden or classical antiquity. References to the golden age before the development of civilization are sometimes indistinguishable from images of mankind before the fall from grace, when people still lived as one with nature" (Milanich and Milbrath 1989, 209). An early eighteenth-century engraving shows the chief of the province of Coosa greeting de Soto and his men (see figure 71). The chief is depicted as larger than life, a god-like figure holding a ceremonial mace. He is being carried on a flower-decked litter preceded by a trumpet blower. Even though the details of the engraving are somewhat erroneous—for example, the horn blower should probably be blowing on a Busycon shell—the artist has captured the great status afforded the elite by their constituents.

Written accounts, such as those of de la Vega, reflect as well an admiration for Native American architecture, describing the artificial mountains, mound-top temples, and impressive palisades with respect. Even though many of these

71. The chief of the Coosa greets De Soto. An engraving from *De Gedenkwaardige van don Ferdinand de Soto* (Leyden: P. Van der Aa, 1706). Courtesy of the W.S. Hoole Special Collections Library, University of Alabama, Tuscaloosa.

accounts allude to the disappointing failure of the effort to find cities with treasuries full of gold and jewels, they nevertheless reflect the impact of the exotic and mysterious world of La Florida on the first European intruders.

The chronicles also indicate the high degree of respect that the Spaniards developed for the skills of Native American warriors. Referring to the expedition of Hernando de Soto, the Spanish historian Lopez de Gomara wrote, "He went about for five years hunting mines, thinking it would be like Peru. He made no settlement, and thus he died, and destroyed those who went with him. Never will conquerors do well unless they settle before they undertake anything else, especially here where the Indians are valiant bowmen and strong" (Milanich and Milbrath 1989, 34).

From the Indians themselves we have only a few incomplete records, mostly from Central and South America, of the impressions made by the Spaniards. "Their faces were not familiar," wrote one Maya, "and the lords took them for gods" (Milanich and Milbrath 1989, 70). "To our Indian eyes," wrote Huaman Poma, a native Inca educated by the Spanish, "the Spaniards looked as if they were shrouded like corpses" (Milanich and Milbrath 1989, 71).

If they were at first taken for gods and treated with respect and awe, the Spaniards soon proved themselves not only ungodlike in their behavior but mortal as well, and the Native Americans' reaction turned from adoration to hostility and contempt. When the survivors of de Soto's ill-fated expedition gave up their quest for riches and fled down the Mississippi River, they were harassed continuously by Native American warriors paddling fleets of dugout canoes. When at last the surviving Spaniards reached the waters of the gulf, a lone Indian stood up in his canoe, shouting and gesturing at them. One of the Indian slaves who accompanied the Spanish translated his words: "If we possessed such large canoes as yours we would follow you to your land and conquer it, for we too are men like yourselves" (Varner and Varner 1980). And a Florida chief, referred to in an account of the de Soto expedition, is quoted as saying, "I have long since learned who you Castillians are. . . . To me you are professional vagabonds who wander from place to place, gaining your livelihood by robbing, sacking and murdering people who have given you no offense" (Varner and Varner 1980).

Many of the Spaniards themselves were horrified by the excesses of the conquistadors. In his book *A Brief Account of the Destruction of the Indies*, printed in Seville in 1552, a Dominican priest, Friar Bartolomé de Las Casas, recounted the atrocities committed by the Spaniards against the people of the New World. While the accuracy of his claims remains a subject of scholarly debate, numerous other accounts, including those of de la Vega, as well as the engravings of such European artists as Theodore De Bry, attest to the cruelty of the Spanish invaders (see figure 72).

72. De Soto's cruelties
in Florida; De Bry in
Benzoni, *Americae*, 1595.
Courtesy of Rare Books
and Manuscripts
Division, The New York
Public Library/Astor,
Lenox, and Tilden
Foundations.

Worse yet, the Indians, despite their extraordinary courage and their legendary cunning in war, were no match for the Europeans' most effective, although unintentional, weapon—Old World diseases (see figure 73). During the two centuries following Columbus's first voyage, epidemics of malaria, smallpox, measles, bubonic plague, and influenza killed millions of Native Americans throughout the Southeast. Towns described as large and flourishing when de Soto passed through them in the mid-1500s were reported as small and pathetic, or abandoned altogether, by members of the Tristan de Luna expedition a mere twenty years later. "Native depopulation in the North American continent during the sixteenth century was severe, especially among peoples who suffered from both Spanish military actions and epidemics. Some of the southeastern Indians first encountered by the Spanish died out in the sixteenth century. . . . In the Southwest, depopulation was widespread as a result of epidemics that came with Spanish contact beginning in 1539. The most accurate records of population decline come from Mexico, where census figures for some communities in the Valley of Mexico indicate that 30 to 50 percent of the people died from epidemics during the first six years after Spanish contact" (Milanich and Milbrath 1989, 52).

In Florida, the Calusa and other Florida Indians were reduced to a handful by the early eighteenth century. Fewer than 1,000 remained of the approxi-

73. Indians curing disease; de Bry after le Moyne, *Brevis narratio*, 1591. Courtesy of Rare Books and Manuscripts Division, The New York Public Library/Astor, Lenox, and Tilden Foundations.

mately 100,000 who had greeted the Spaniards in 1513. These remaining individuals were further threatened by various northern tribes, mainly Creeks and Yamassees, who moved into Florida as a result of European pressures farther to the north.

Mississippian civilization, whose roots lay deep in the heartland of the American Bottoms and whose influence once ruled most of the eastern half of the North American continent, was all but eradicated by the dual effects of military conquest and recurring epidemics. The great cities, like Etowah and Moundville, which had continued to blossom in the late stages of Mississippian cultural influence, could not withstand the onslaught of European penetration. European weapons and European diseases provided the coup de grace to the last vestiges of Mississippian domination, and the old towns crumbled into ruins, their wooden temples and statuary turning to dust, their wide plazas covered with weeds. The fields of corn disappeared, the network of trade fell apart, and the production of artifacts associated with the Southeastern Ceremonial Complex ceased.

"Ancestral spirits, sacred landscapes, and communication with the forces of nature are shared American Indian attitudes," writes Richard F. Townsend of the Art Institute of Chicago. "I think they are ultimately deeply rooted in Paleolithic life.... Every rock, every tree, every cave and gully is a place invested with memories of origin times and the deeds of ancestors, mythological heros, and adventures of the tribe.... The land [itself] is their icon, and they have invested it with layers of meaning" (Stuart 1988, 17).

The temple mound was a sacred mountain linking heaven and earth, and the chief was the intermediary between the people and the spiritual beings who ruled the cosmos. His position of leadership was assured by his blood ties with the ancestors, the ancient ones who had formulated the rules and established the rituals in a time so distantly past that no one could remember when The Way It Is had not been so. The people followed the cycle of the seasons, and the seasons followed the movement of the sun. The wheel of time moved slowly in those days. Until the arrival of the black doves, the Mississippian way had persisted in the Southeast for nearly a thousand years.

As we drive through the southeastern United States today, enjoying the verdant landscape and following the paths of the slow-moving rivers, we would do well to remember that the history of the region did not begin with the arrival of the Europeans. The occupation and development of the Southeast by American Indians stretches back at least to 12,000 B.C. When the great earthen mounds of Cahokia were being built by the people of the Mississippian heartland, London was still a provincial outpost in an abandoned Roman colony and Charlemagne had not yet been crowned emperor of Western Europe.

American history is not what we once assumed it to be. It is deeper, richer, and more ancient. In this nation of immigrants, we should never forget our debt to those First Americans who discovered a New World and walked lightly, century after century, on its virgin soil. The Indians are the grandmothers and grandfathers of all Americans, the old ones who have gone before. Their ancient wisdom and their knowledge of the ways of nature, their deep and abiding reverence for this land, and their faith in its abundant resources can provide us with the blueprint for a new American Dream—a vision of the land as something to be cherished and sustained, to be venerated and cared for so that we can finally begin to live in harmony with the sacred land that we inherited from our Indian ancestors. It is not yet too late for us to turn away from greed and recklessness and begin the task of healing and regeneration.

So go to the Old Towns and the Old Fields and listen carefully to what they have to tell you. You may be surprised to find that for all of us, the discovery of America has just begun.

Bibliography

Adair, James. *History of the American Indians.* London, 1775.

Allerton, David, George M. Lauer, and Robert S. Carr. "Ceremonial Tablets and Related Objects from Florida." *Florida Anthropologist* 37, no. 1 (1984).

Bartram, William. *The Travels of William Bartram.* New Haven: Yale University Press, 1958.

Bourne, Edward E., ed. *Narratives of the Career of Hernando de Soto.* New York: A. S. Barnes, 1904.

Brain, Jeffrey P. "The Great Mound Robbery." *Archaeology Magazine* (May/June 1988): 19–28.

———. *Winterville, Late Prehistoric Culture Contact in the Lower Mississippi Valley.* Archaeology Report no. 23. Jackson: Mississippi Department of Archives and History, 1989.

Brose, David S. "The Woodland Period." In *Ancient Art of the American Woodland Indians,* by David S. Brose et al. New York: Harry N. Abrams, Inc., 1985.

Brown, James A. "The Artifacts." Spiro Studies, vol. 4, *Third Annual Report of Caddoan Archaeology.* Norman: University of Oklahoma Research Institute, 1976.

———. "The Mississippian Period." In *Ancient Art of the American Woodland Indians,* by David S. Brose et al. New York: Harry N. Abrams, Inc., 1985.

———. "On Style Divisions of a Southeastern Ceremonial Complex: A Revisionist Perspective." In *The Southeastern Ceremonial Complex,* edited by Patricia Galloway. Lincoln: University of Nebraska Press, 1989.

Brown, Joseph Epes. *Seeing with a Native Eye: Essays on Native American Religion,* edited by Walter Holden Capps. New York: Harper and Row, Inc., 1976.

———. *The Sacred Pipe.* Baltimore: Penguin Books, 1971.

Brown, Virginia Pounds, and Laurella Owen. *Southern Indian Myths and Legends.* Birmingham: Beechwood Books, 1985.

Bullen, Ripley. "The Famous Crystal River Site." *Florida Anthropologist* 6, no. 1 (1953).

Burland, Cottie. *North American Indian Mythology.* New York: Paul Hamlyn, 1965.

Chapman, Jefferson. *Tellico Archaeology, 12,000 Years of Native American History.* Knoxville: University of Tennessee Press, 1985.

———. *The Archaeological Collections at the Frank H. McClung Museum.* Occasional Paper #7, Frank H. McClung Museum. Knoxville: University of Tennessee, 1988.

Coe, Michael, Dean Snow, and Elizabeth Benson. *Atlas of Ancient America.* New York: Facts on File Publications, 1986.

Conrad, Lawrence A. "The Southeastern Ceremonial Complex on the Northern Middle Mississippi Frontier: Late Prehistoric Politico-religious Systems in the Central Illinois River Valley." In *The Southeastern Ceremonial Complex,* edited by Patricia Galloway. Lincoln: University of Nebraska Press, 1989.

Cordell, Ann S. "Ceramic Technology at a Weeden Island Period Archaeological Site in North Florida." Ceramic Notes #2, Occasional Papers of the Ceramic Technology Lab, Florida State Museum. Gainesville: Florida State Museum, University of Florida, 1984.

Cotterill, R. S. *The Southern Indians.* Civilization of the American Indian Series. Norman: University of Oklahoma Press, 1954.

Cronyn, George W., ed. *American Indian Poetry.* New York: Ballantine Books, 1962.

Crutchfield, James A. *The Natchez Trace: A Pictorial History.* Nashville: Rutledge Hill Press, 1985.

Dickens, Roy S. "Of Sky and Earth, Art of the Early Southeastern Indians." Exhibition catalogue. Atlanta: High Museum of Art, 1982.

Emerson, Thomas E. *Mississippian Stone Images in Illinois.* Illinois Archaeological Survey, Circular #6. Champaign-Urbana: University of Illinois, 1982.

Engle, Nancy. "Prehistoric Figurines of the Eastern United States and Their Significance." Master's thesis, University of Illinois, 1957.

Fagan, Brian M. *People of the Earth: An Introduction to World Prehistory.* Boston: Little, Brown and Company, 1985.

Fairbanks, Charles H. *Archaeology of the Funeral Mound, Ocmulgee National Monument, Georgia.* Archaeological Research Series #3. Washington, D.C.: National Park Service, 1956.

Ferrell, Keith. "An Interview with Morris Berman." *Omni Magazine* (August 1991).

Ford, James A. "Early Formative Cultures in Georgia and Florida." *American Antiquity* 31, no. 6 (1966).

Ford, James A., and Clarence H. Webb. *Poverty Point, a Late Archaic Site in Louisiana.* Anthropological Papers, vol. 46, pt. 1. New York: American Museum of Natural History, 1956.

Fowler, Melvin L. *Cahokia: Ancient Capital of the Midwest.* Addison-Wesley Module in Anthropology no. 48. Menlo Park, Calif.: Cummings Publications, 1974.

Fundaburk, Emma Lila, and Mary Douglas Fundaburk Foreman. *Sun Circles and Human Hands.* Luverne, Ala.: Emma Lila Fundaburk, Publisher, 1957.

Galloway, Patricia, ed. *The Southeastern Ceremonial Complex: Artifacts and Analysis.* Lincoln: University of Nebraska Press, 1989.

Garcilaso de la Vega, El Inca. *See* Varner, John, and Jeannette Varner.

Gilliland, Marion Spjut. *The Material Culture of Key Marco.* Gainesville: University Presses of Florida, 1975.

———. *Key Marco's Buried Treasure: Archaeology and Adventure in the Nineteenth Century.* Gainesville: University Press of Florida, 1989.

Goggin, John. *Some Pottery Types from Central Florida.* Gainesville Anthropological Association Bulletin #1 (1948).

Griffin, James, ed. *Archaeology of the Eastern United States.* Chicago: University of Chicago Press, 1952.

———. *The Chronological Position of the Hopewellian Culture in the Eastern United States.*

Museum of Anthropology Anthropological Papers #12. Ann Arbor: University of Michigan, 1958.

Griffin, James, and William McKern. "Painted Pottery Figurines from Illinois." *American Antiquity* 10, no. 3 (1945).

Hall, Robert. "The Cultural Background of Mississippian Symbolism." In *The Southeastern Ceremonial Complex,* edited by Patricia Galloway. Lincoln: University of Nebraska Press, 1989.

Haltkrantz, Ake. *Native Religions of North America.* San Francisco: HarperCollins Publishers, 1987.

Hancock, William. "Chucalissa." Chucalissa Archaeological Site, brochure. Memphis, Tenn.: n.d.

Harrington, Spencer P. M. "The Looting of Arkansas." *Archaeology Magazine* (May/June 1991).

Highwater, Jamake. *The Primal Mind.* New York: New American Library, 1981.

Hudson, Charles M. *Four Centuries of Southern Indians.* Athens: University of Georgia Press, 1975.

Jones, B. Calvin. "Southern Cult Manifestations at the Lake Jackson Site, Leon County, Florida: Salvage Excavation of Mound 3." *Midcontinental Journal of Archaeology* 7, no. 1 (1982).

Klein, Cecelia F. "Depictions of the Dispossessed." *Art Journal* 49, no. 2 (1990).

Knaufelt, David A. *American Tropic.* New York: Simon and Schuster, Inc., 1986.

Knight, Vernon J., Jr. "Some Speculations on Mississippian Monsters." In *The Southeastern Ceremonial Complex,* edited by Patricia Galloway. Lincoln: University of Nebraska Press, 1989.

Kopper, Philip. *The Smithsonian Book of North American Indians Before the Coming of the Europeans.* Washington, D.C.: Smithsonian Books, 1986.

Larson, Lewis H., Jr. "The Etowah Site." In *The Southeastern Ceremonial Complex,* edited by Patricia Galloway. Lincoln: University of Nebraska Press, 1989.

Lathrap, D. W. "Our Father the Cayman, Our Mother the Gourd: Spinden Revisited, or a Unitary Model for the Emergence of Agriculture in the New World." In *Origins of Agriculture,* edited by C. Reed. The Hague: 1977.

Laudonnière, René. *Three Voyages.* Translated by Charles E. Bennett. Gainesville: University Press of Florida, 1975.

Lazarus, Yulee W. "The Buck Burial Mound: A Mound of the Weeden Island Culture." Fort Walton Beach, Fla.: Temple Mound Museum, 1979.

Lewis, Thomas M. N., and Madeline Kneberg. *Hiwassee Island, An Archaeological Account of Four Tennessee Indian Peoples.* Knoxville: University of Tennessee Press, 1946.

———. *Tribes that Slumber: Indians of the Tennessee Region.* Knoxville: University of Tennessee Press, 1958.

Marshall, Richard A. "Indians of Mississippi: An Archaeological Perspective." Starkville: Cobb Institute of Archaeology, Mississippi State University, n.d.

McDonald, Jerry N., and Susan L. Woodward. *Indian Mounds of the Atlantic Coast.* Newark, Ohio: McDonald and Woodward Publishing Company, 1987.

McMichael, E. *Vera Cruz, the Crystal River Complex, and the Hopewellian Climax.* Hopewellian Studies, Illinois State Museum Scientific Papers 12. Springfield, 1964.

Mereness, Newton D., ed. "Ranger's Report of Travels with General Oglethorpe." In *Travels in the American Colonies.* New York: 1916.

Milanich, Jerald T. *Life in a Ninth-Century Indian Household, a Weeden Island Indian Fall-Winter Site on the Upper Apalachicola River, Florida.* Bureau of Historic Properties Bulletin #4. Tallahassee: Florida Department of State, 1974.

Milanich, Jerald T., and Charles Fairbanks. *Florida Archaeology.* Orlando: Academic Press, 1980.

Milanich, Jerald T., A. S. Cordell, V. J. Knight, Jr., T. A. Kohler, and B. S. Sigler-Lavelle. *McKeithen Weeden Island: The Culture of North Florida, A.D. 200–900.* Orlando: Academic Press, 1984.

Milanich, Jerald T., and Susan Milbrath, eds. *First Encounters: Spanish Explorations in the Caribbean and the United States, 1492–1570.* Gainesville: University Press of Florida, 1989.

Moore, Alexander, ed. *Nairne's Muskhogean Journals, the 1708 Expedition to the Mississippi River.* Jackson: University Press of Mississippi, 1988.

Moore, Clarence B. "Aboriginal Sites on the Tennessee River." *Journal of the Academy of Natural Sciences* 16 (1915): 169–428.

Morgan, William N. *Prehistoric Architecture in the Eastern United States.* Cambridge: MIT Press, 1980.

Nabokov, Peter, and Robert Easton. *Native American Architecture.* New York: Oxford University Press, 1989.

Neihardt, John G. *Black Elk Speaks.* Lincoln: University of Nebraska Press, 1969.

Neitzel, Robert S. *The Grand Village of the Natchez Revisited.* Archaeological Report #12. Jackson: Mississippi Department of Archives and History, 1983.

O'Connor, Mallory McCane. "Grave Goods of the Florida Elite." In *Phoebus 4,* edited by Anthony Lacy Gully. Phoenix: Arizona State University, 1985.

Penney, David W. "The Late Archaic Period." In *Ancient Art of the American Woodland Indians* by David S. Brose et al. New York: Harry N. Abrams, Inc., 1985.

Peterson, Dennis A. "A History of Excavations and Interpretations of Artifacts from the Spiro Mound Site." In *The Southeastern Ceremonial Complex,* edited by Patricia Galloway. Lincoln: University of Nebraska Press, 1989.

Pfeiffer, John E. "Indian City on the Mississippi." In *Time-Life Natural Science Annual.* New York: Time-Life Books, Inc., 1974.

Phillips, Philip, and James A. Brown. *Pre-Columbian Shell Engravings from the Craig Mound at Spiro, Oklahoma, Part I.* Cambridge: Peabody Museum Press, Harvard University, 1978.

Pope, G. D., Jr. *Ocmulgee National Monument—Georgia.* National Park Service Historical Handbook, Series #24. Washington, D.C., 1956.

Prufer, Olaf H. "The Hopewell Cult." *Scientific American Magazine* (June 1964).

Putnam, F. W. "Archaeological Explorations in Tennessee." *Eleventh Annual Report of the Trustees of the Peabody Museum* 2 (1878).

Rubin, Arnold. *Art as Technology,* edited by Zena Pearlstone. Beverly Hills: Hillcrest Press, 1989.

Sears, William H. *Excavations at Kolomoki, Final Report.* University of Georgia Series in Anthropology #5. Athens: University of Georgia Press, 1956.

———. *Fort Center: An Archaeological Site in the Lake Okeechobee Basin.* Gainesville: University Press of Florida, 1982.

Shetrone, Henry. *The Mound Builders.* New York: Appleton Century Croft, 1930.

Silverberg, Robert. *The Mound Builders.* Greenwich, Conn.: New York Graphic Society, 1970.

Squier, E. G., and E. H. Davis. *Ancient Monuments of the Mississippi Valley.* Washington, D.C.: Smithsonian Institution, 1848.

Stuart, G. S. *America's Ancient Cities.* Washington, D.C.: National Geographic Society, 1988.

Stuart, George E. *Discovering Man's Past in the Americas.* Washington, D.C.: National Geographic Society, 1973.

Swanton, John R. *Indian Tribes of the Lower Mississippi Valley and Adjacent Coast of the Gulf of Mexico.* Bureau of American Ethnology, Bulletin #43. Washington, D.C.: Smithsonian Institution, 1911.

———. *Early History of the Creek Indians and Their Neighbors.* Bulletin 73. Washington: Bureau of American Ethnology, 1922.

———. *The Indians of the Southern United States.* Bureau of American Ethnology, Bulletin #137. Washington, D.C.: Smithsonian. Institution, 1946.

Thomas, Cyrus. *Report on the Mound Explorations of the Bureau of Ethnology.* Bureau of American Ethnology, 12th Annual Report. Washington, D.C.: Smithsonian Institution, 1894.

Thomas, David H. "Part One: The World as It Was." In *The Native Americans,* edited by Betty Ballantine and Ian Ballantine. Atlanta: Turner Publishing, Inc., 1993.

Thwaites, Reuben G., ed. *The Jesuit Relations and Allied Documents: Travels and Explorations of the Jesuit Missionaries in New France, 1610–1791.* New York: Pageant Books, 1959.

Tocqueville, Alexis de. *Democracy in America.* Vol. 1. Translated by Henry Reeve. New York: Random House, 1945.

Toffler, Alvin, and Heidi Toffler. "War, Wealth and a New Era in History." *World Monitor Magazine* (May 1991).

Townsend, Richard F., ed. *The Ancient Americas: Art from Sacred Landscapes.* Chicago: Art Institute of Chicago Press, 1992.

Trevelyan, Amelia. "Powhatan Copper and the Prehistoric Ceremonial Complexes of the Eastern United States." In *Phoebus 4,* edited by Anthony Lacy Gully. Phoenix: Arizona State University, 1989.

Varner, John, and Jeannette Varner, trans. and eds. *The Florida of the Inca,* by El Inca Garcilaso de la Vega. Austin: University of Texas Press, 1980.

Viola, Herman J. *After Columbus: The Smithsonian Chronicles of the North American Indians.* New York: Orion Books, 1990.

Walker, Bryce. *Earthquake.* Alexandria, Va.: Time-Life Books, Inc., 1980.

Walthall, John A., and Joseph O. Vogel. *Moundville, an Introduction to a Mississippian Chiefdom.* Nature Notebook no. 8. Tuscaloosa: Alabama Museum of Natural History, University of Alabama, 1982.

Weatherford, Jack. *Native Roots: How the Indians Enriched America.* New York: Crown Publishers, 1991.

Webb, Malcolm C. "Functional and Historical Parallelisms between Mesoamerican and Mississippian Cultures." In *The Southeastern Ceremonial Complex,* edited by Patricia Galloway. Lincoln: University of Nebraska Press, 1989.

Webb, William. *The Adena People.* Columbus: Ohio Historical Society, Ohio State University Press, 1957.

Widmer, Randolph J. "The Relationship of Ceremonial Artifacts from South Florida with the Southeastern Ceremonial Complex." In *The Southeastern Ceremonial Complex,* edited by Patricia Galloway. Lincoln: University of Nebraska Press, 1989.

Wiley, Gordon. *Archaeology of the Florida Gulf Coast.* Smithsonian Miscellaneous Collections 113. Washington, D.C.: Smithsonian Institution, 1949.

Index

Page numbers in bold refer to illustrations.

Berman, Morris, 53

Big boy–effigy pipe (Spiro site), 58–59, 70, **plate 10;** origin of, 78

Bi-lobed arrows, 59, 102; in costume, 70–71, 131

Birds: in creation myths, 3; in Mississippian art, 46, 119. *See also* Effigies, bird; Falcons; Raptors

Birdstones, 11

Birger figurine, 34, 35, 60, **plate 8;** place of origin, 63, 78

Black Drink Ceremony, 136

Black Elk (Lakota holy man), 72

Black Warrior River, 98

Boskita (summer ceremony), 73–74, 121

Braden style (Mississippian art), 72

Brain, Jeffrey, 62, 84, 85, 87

Brose, David, 14, 54, 71, 80; on climatic shifts, 79

Brown, James, 57, 63, 75; on ancestor cult, 48; on burial customs, 108, 112–13; on Etowah, 113; on Mississippian art, 72; on symbolism, 34

Buck Mound site (Florida): burial urns of, 69, **plate 3;** effigies of, 20, 22–23

Bullen, Ripley, 134

Burial customs: of Adena culture, 13; of Hopewell culture, 17; Mississippian, 45, 54, 64–65, 108; of Safety Harbor culture, 133; of St. Johns culture, 126–27. *See also* Death

Burial mounds, 107; of Cahokia, 28–29, 45, 49, 97, **plate 6;** of Kolomoki site, **plate 4;** of Lake Jackson site, 129–31; layout of, 108; of Ocmulgee site, 115, **116;** of Safety Harbor culture, 133–34; of Shiloh site, 77; of St. Johns culture, 126. *See also* Ceremonial centers; Mounds

Busk (summer ceremony), 73–74, 121

Caddoan people, 61; ancestor cult of, 111; warrior cult of, 80

Cadle, Cornelius, 77

Cahokia: agriculture of, 29–30, 31, 49–50; artifacts of, 28, 30–31, 34, 72; civilization of, 24–25; demise of, 49–50; effigies of, 37, 46; exports of, 30–31; geology of, 50; influence on Mississippian culture, 51, 86–87; pipe effigies of, 39–42; sociopolitical life of, 28; suburbs of, 29–30; trade networks of, 30–31, 51. *See also* Mississippian culture

Cahokia (city), xv, 145; architecture of, xv; fortifications of, **plate 7,** 29; founding of, 27; layout of, 27–29; Monks Mound of, **26,** 27, 28, 44, **47;** Mound 72 of,

45, 49, 97, **plate 6;** plazas of, 28; sun circles of, 29

Calendar circles, 9–10

Calos (Calusa town), xv, 135–36

Calusa people: demise of, 140, 143–44; Mississippian influence on, 135, 136–37; trade with Apalachee, 137

Capaha people, 113

Capes, feathered, 68–69, 71; of Lake Jackson site, 131

Captives, effigies of, 91–92, **93**

Carolinas, Mississippian culture in, 119, 122–23

Casas, Bartolomé de las, 142

Casquin people, 113

Cat figure (Key Marco site), 140, **plate 32**

Ceramics: Adena, 13; of Coles Creek culture, 85–86; of Fort Walton culture, **plate 30;** of Late Archaic period, 11–12; of Moundville site, 101–2, **103;** of Poverty Point site, 9; of Safety Harbor culture, 137; of Stallings Island site, 11

Ceremonial centers: abandonment of, 97; of Cahokia, 24, 27, 28–29, 49; of Chucalissa, 67–68; of Emerald site, 90; of Lake Jackson site, 129–30, 131; of Ocmulgee site, 115; of Shiloh, 77; of Spiro site, 60, **61;** of Town Creek site, 122; of Winterville site, 84. *See also* Burial mounds; Mounds

Ceremonialism: decline of, 55; Hopewell, 17–18, 20; Mississippian, 71, 118; and seasonal cycles, 24–25. *See also* Rituals

Charlevoix, 67

Charnel houses, 109; of Cahokia, 28–29, **plate 6;** effigy posts of, **21;** of Spiro site, 60

Cherokees, corn mythology of, 36

Chickasaw Indians, 56

Chiefs: of Moundville society, 97, 100, 104, 105; role in ancestor cult, 111, 144–45; of South Florida, 136

Children, effigies of, 37, **38**

Choctaw Indians, 67

Chucalissa (Mississippian city), 67–68, **69, 70**

Chunkey players: attributes of, 58; costume of, 75; effigies of, 75, **plate 11;** in Mississippian art, 71

Chunkey stones, **74,** 75

Citico site (Tennessee), 119

Climate, changes in, 49–50, 78

Coe, Joeffrey L., 119–20

Coles Creek culture, 84; Mississippian influence on, 87; pottery of, 85–86

Coosa people, 121; Citico style of, 81; meeting with de Soto, **141**

Safety Harbor culture, 125, 133–34; pottery of, 137, **plate 30**

Safety Harbor site (Florida), **134, plate 31**

Sawyer, Wells, 140

Schild pipe, 36, **37**

Scioto Valley (Ohio), Hopewell culture of, 16

Sears, William, 115

Sea turtle head (Key Marco site), 138, **139**

Serpents, symbolism of, 48

Shell engravings: Citico style of, 81; of Etowah site, 115; of Fort Walton culture, **plate 29;** Mississippian, 56, 119; of Spiro site, 34, 62–63, 69; of St. Johns culture, 127

Shell middens, 135

Shiloh pipe, 77–78, **plate 14**

Shiloh site (Tenn.), 75, **78, 79, 80, plate 13;** fortifications of, 77; mounds of, **plate 12**

Silverberg, Robert, 6, 17

Skull motifs, 102, **103**

Social status: iconography of, 4; in Mississippian culture, 31, 49; of Natchez Indians, 95–96, 97; of warriors, 56. *See also* Hierarchy

Southeast: agriculture in, 53; artistic history of, xv; excavation sites of, **8, 54**

Southeastern Ceremonial Complex: demise of, 144; Etowah artifacts of, 115; in Florida, 128; religious beliefs of, 55, 72; spread of, 80; symbolism of, 75. *See also* South Florida Ceremonial Complex

Southern Cult. *See* Southeastern Ceremonial Complex

South Florida Ceremonial Complex, 136

Spaniards, atrocities by, 142, **143**

Spiro Mounds Archaeological State Park, 64

Spiro site (Oklahoma): ancestor effigies of, 111; ceremonial center of, 60, **61;** copper artifacts at, 125, 131; costumes at, 69; gorgets of, 119; human effigies of, 34; looting of, 63–64; Phase III of, 61; shell engravings of, 34, 62–63, 69; trade networks of, 61, 62; warrior effigies of, 60

St. Johns culture, 125–29

St. Johns River, Hopewell sites of, 20

Stallings Island site (Georgia), 11

Stirling, Matthew, 134

Stockades. *See* Fortifications

Stone pallets, **14,** 100, 102, **104;** of Etowah site, 115

Stupas, Indian, 4

Sun circles: of Cahokia, 29; motifs of, 71

Sun worship, 10, 59, 108

Swanton, John, 75

Swift Creek people, 115

Symbolism: of agriculture, 34–36; of animals, 32; of eyes, 49, 57, 71, 100, 101, 102, 118, 128; Mississippian, 32, 34, 40, 48–49, 57, 59, 71–72

T. O. Fuller State Park (Tenn.), 67–68

Talwa (town), 120, 121

Tascalusa people, costume of, 68

Tattooed Serpent (Natchez Chief), 96

Technology, art as, 10

Temple mounds. *See* Burial mounds; Ceremonial centers; Mounds

Tennessee, Mississippian settlements in, 118

Tennessee River, **plate 13**

Thomas, Cyrus, 89

Thomas, David, 35

Thursby site (Florida), 128; totems at, 129

Timucuan people, 97

Tobacco, use during Woodland period, 12

Toffler, Alvin, 53

Toltec, ball games of, 72

Totems, 129, **130**

Town Creek site (North Carolina), 119–20, **122;** reconstruction of, 121–22, **plates 23–27**

Townsend, Richard F., xv, 144

Trade networks: of Cahokia, 30–31; of Hopewell peoples, 17, 22, 23; of Late Archaic period, 10–11; of Spiro site, 61

Trevelyan, Amelia, 48, 100

Trophy heads, 44, 45

Tuberculosis, 38

Uktenas (underwater panthers), 33–34

Underworld, in Mississippian culture, 34, 39, 102

Vogel, Joseph, 100, 103–4

Warfare: effect of agriculture on, 53, 55–56; in Mississippian art, 32, 48

Warriors: cult of, 48, 60, 80; Mississippian, 55–56; status of, 56. *See also* Effigies, warrior

Water-creatures: in creation myths, 3; paintings of, 33–34

Weatherford, Jack, xiv